Inclusive Schooling Practices:
Pedagogical and Research Foundations

A Synthesis of the Literature that Informs
Best Practices about Inclusive Schooling

Policy   Practice

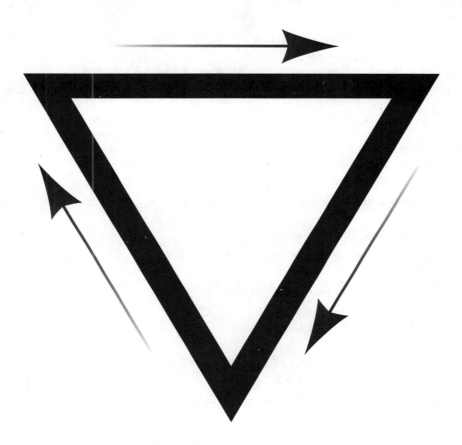

Research

Gail McGregor, Ed.D.
Consortium on Inclusive Schooling Practices
The University of Montana - Rural Institute on Disabilities

R. Timm Vogelsberg, Ph.D.
The University of Montana - Rural Institute on Disabilities

Distributed exclusively by Paul H. Brookes Publishing Co., Inc.

Table of Contents

Inclusive Schooling Practices: Pedagogical and Research Foundations 5

Part I: Inclusion in the Age of School Restructuring 6

Innovation and Change in Education 6
    Table 1. Barriers to Educational Change 8

The Nature of Inclusive Schools 9
    Table 2. Common Misperceptions about Inclusion 10

Applying Lessons about Change to Inclusion 11
    Table 3. Strategies to Facilitate Inclusion Derived from Change Literature 12

Part II: Educational Structures and Practices that Support Diversity 15

Responsive Instructional Practices 15
    Table 4. Models that Describe Differences in Learning Style 17

Strategies to Accommodate Specific Barriers to Learning 18

Creating Caring and Supportive Learning Communities 21

    Table 5. Child Development Project's Essential Ingredients to
    Promote Community Building 23
    Table 6. Small Group Structures that Encourage Collaboration
    in Heterogeneous Groups 23
    Table 7. Collaborative Skills that can be Promoted through
    Small Group Learning 26

Organizational Structures that Support Responsive Schooling Practices. 27

    Table 8. Block Scheduling Models 29
    Table 9. Strategies to Find Time to Collaborate 32

Summary 33
    Table 10. Indicators of Learner Centeredness 33

Part III: Research about Inclusive Schooling Practices 37

Perceptions of Key Stakeholders about Inclusion 37

Parent Perspectives 38
Teacher Perspectives 39
Student Perspectives 41

Responses to Accommodating Differences in the Classroom 43

Evolution of Models to Support General Education Teachers 44

Consulting Teacher Models 44
Collaborative Consultation 46
Co-Teaching 46

Research about the Implementation Process 47

Multi-Site Studies 48
Table 11. Advice Themes for School Personnel Adopting an Inclusive Model 48
Building Level Implementation Efforts 48
Table 12. Case Studies Focused on Building Level Change 49
Table 13. Case Study Observations as Compared to Inclusion "Best Practices" 50
District Level Implementation Efforts 53
Table 14. District Level Inclusion Implementation Studies-Descriptions 54

Outcomes of Inclusive Schooling Practices 57

Skill Acquisition for Students with Disabilities 57

Social Outcomes for Students with Disabilities 60

Impact on Students without Disabilities 63

Impact on Parents 66

Impact on Teachers 68

Program-Related Outcomes 69

Concluding Observations and Future Directions 70

References 73

Appendices

    Appendix A: Federal Appellate Court Decisions A-1

    Appendix B: Literature Review Table . . . . .B

        Table B-1: Documented Outcomes for Students with Disabilities in
                Inclusive Settings B-1
        Table B-2: Documented Outcomes for Students without Disabilities
                in Inclusive Settings B-21
        Table B-3: Documented Outcomes for Parents Associated with
                Inclusive Settings B-28
        Table B-4: Outcomes and Behaviors of Teachers in Inclusive Settings B-36
        Table B-5: Programmatic and Administrative Outcomes of Inclusive Schooling . . .B-44

Inclusive Schooling Practices:
Pedagogical and Research Foundations

Almost twenty-five years after the publication of <u>A Nation at Risk</u> (National Commission on Excellence in Education, 1983), initiatives to improve America's schools dominate the educational agenda at the national, state, and local levels. Policymakers and educators continue to grapple with issues of equity and excellence as schools struggle to define and achieve high performance standards within a context of declining budgets and an increasingly diverse (Astuto, Clark, Read, McGree & Fernandez, 1994) and economically disadvantaged (Polakow, 1992) student population. Despite these challenges, schools *are* being successfully re-created across this country, becoming communities that are "learner-centered, enriched by teachers' learning opportunities, and supported by assessment practices that inspire continuous improvement" (Lieberman, 1995, pg. 1).

To a growing extent, the needs of *all* students, including those with disabilities, are becoming a part of school restructuring agendas (e.g., Katsiyannis, Conderman, & Franks, 1995; National Center on Educational Restructuring and Inclusion, 1994, 1995; Roach, 1995). This perspective is illustrated in the words of staff from a rural school district in Oregon:

> *Our school district does not view inclusion as a <u>program</u> [emphasis added]. It is part of our total belief and practice. It goes part and parcel with the idea that our responsibility is to all children. If inclusion is only used as a way to deal with special education students, it will never accomplish anything* (Ontario, Oregon School District, National Center on Educational Restructuring and Inclusion, 1995, pg. 268).

As reflected in these comments, the inclusion of students with disabilities is not merely an issue of a student's physical placement. The presence of students with disabilities in general education classrooms stimulates educators to consider the match between classroom climate, curriculum, teaching practices, and the needs of students with identified learning differences (Sapon-Shevin, 1994/95). Although students labeled as exceptional do not represent the only source of diversity in the general education classroom, their presence provides a catalyst for teachers to consider the diverse learning needs of *all* of their students in the design of instructional activities.

The purpose of this monograph is to summarize the literature base that informs our current understanding of the best approaches to support students with disabilities in inclusive settings. As described by Cooper (1989), the search for and selection of literature to include in this synthesis was guided by a *conceptual definition*. In this case, the concept of *informing our current understanding about inclusive schooling practices* was operationally defined as literature that addresses adoption processes, implementation practices, and outcomes of inclusive schooling. This "wide net" approach led to theoretical literature about the change process as it relates to school reform and restructuring, pedagogical literature from the special and general education fields that focuses on strategies to accommodate diverse learners in the general education classroom, and empirical literature about the impact of inclusion. A concerted effort was made to consider literature both supportive and critical of inclusion, since lessons can be derived from both positive and negative exemplars.

The resulting information base is organized into three parts. In Part I, a context is established by considering the movement toward inclusive schooling practices within the larger arena of educational change and school reform. This is followed by a synthesis of information about instructional practices (Part II) that support diverse students. Finally, Part III summarizes available research about inclusion. This includes research that informs implementation efforts, as well as studies which examine outcomes.

Part I:
Inclusion in the Age of School Restructuring

> *The view that underpins the new paradigm for school reform starts from the assumptions that students are not standardized and that teaching is not routine* (Darling-Hammond, 1993, pg. 757).

Over the last decade, the terminology used to describe school improvement efforts has shifted from talk of school reform to that of school restructuring. This change reflects the growing awareness that top-down reform measures focused on improving the efficiency and effectiveness of existing educational structures are insufficient to achieve desired improvements in student learning and performance. Restructuring is future-focused (Whitaker & Moses, 1994), based on new ways of thinking about the primary purpose of education. The extent to which inclusion is ultimately a part of the fabric of restructured schools is linked to the success of efforts to transform philosophical assumptions into practice. Understanding the process of change in educational settings is essential in guiding this work.

Innovation and Change in Education

Stimulated by educators like Larry Cuban (1988a,b), all struggling with issues of school reform, Fullan (1991) asked the question "How it is that so much school reform has taken place over the last century yet schooling appears pretty much the same as it's always been (pg. 29)? It is helpful to consider this perspective relative to the substantial literature base addressing the issue of change in schools.

Hargreaves (1997a) recently summarized over a decade of study of educational change, including the work of Newmann and Wehlage (1995), Miles and colleagues (Louis & Miles, 1990; Miles & Huberman, 1984), Seymour Sarason (1990), his own work with Michael Fullan (Fullan, 1991, 1993; Fullan & Hargreaves, 1996; Hargreaves, 1994; Hargreaves, Early & Ryan, 1996), and others involved in this area (e.g., McLaughlin, 1990; Rudduck, 1991; Stoll & Fink, 1996). Based on this rich body of literature, he distilled nine factors that are associated with unsuccessful attempts to change educational practice. These factors are identified and defined in Table 1.

Given this extensive list of potentially "fatal" flaws, the prospect of educational change does seem to be aptly captured in Fullan's remarks. Eight years later, however, Cuban challenges the pervasive myth that "schools hardly ever change", writing:

> *Such a myth is not only mistaken but is also the basis for the profound pessimism that presently exists over the capacity of public schools to improve. The fact is that over the last century, there have been many organizational, governance, curricular, and even instructional changes in public schools. Such changes have been adopted, adapted, implemented, and institutionalized* (Cuban, 1996, pg. 75).

He cites new subject offerings in the school curriculum, the presence of students with disabilities in public schools, and consolidation of small high schools into larger ones as evidence that schools do, in fact, change.

Establishing the distinction between *incremental* and *fundamental* change provides language and an operational standard to talk about this phenomena and, perhaps, reconcile these seemingly conflicting opinions. Incremental changes are innovations that improve the efficiency and effectiveness of existing structures; fundamental changes alter the very structure or organization of a system (Cuban, 1996). The introduction of AIDS education within the existing health curriculum is an incremental change, while the adoption of a multi-grade organizational schema represents a fundamental change. Similarly, increasing the amount of time a student with a mild disability spends in the general education classroom is an incremental change. **Delivering special education supports to all students with disabilities in a manner that begins with the assumption of regular class placement represents a fundamental change for many schools in this country.**

If inclusion is to become a fundamental change in schools, available lessons regarding the adoption of educational innovations must be heeded. All too often, service delivery for students with disabilities has been considered a peripheral issue, one that can be handled within the special education structures of the school. While collaboration with general education is acknowledged in principle, the underlying structures that enable this to occur are not in place. To date, special educators have not been integral players in discussions of school reform (Lilly, 1987; Sage & Burrello, 1994). Lessons about educational change suggest that it is incumbent upon them to do so.

Table 1
Barriers to Educational Change

Barrier	Why Change Does Not Succeed[1]
Rationale	The reason for the change is poorly conceptualized or not clearly demonstrated. It is not obvious who will benefit and how. What the change will achieve for students in particular is not spelled out.
Scope	The change is too broad and ambitious so that teachers have to work on too many fronts, or it is too limited and specific so that little real change occurs at all.
Pace	The change is too fast for people to cope with, or too slow so that they come impatient or bored and move on to something else.
Resources	The change is poorly resourced or resources are withdrawn once the first flush of innovation is over. There is not enough money for materials or time for teachers to plan. The change is built on the back of teachers, who cannot bear it for long without additional support.
Commitment	There is no long-term commitment to the change to carry people through the anxiety, frustration, and despair of early experimentation and unavoidable setbacks.
Key Staff	Key staff who can contribute to the change, or might be affected by it, are not committed, Conversely, key staff might be over involved as an administrative or innovative elite, from which other teachers feel excluded. Resistance and resentment are the consequences in either case.
Parents	Parents oppose the change because they are kept at a distance from it. Professionals can collaborate so enthusiastically among themselves that they involve the community too little or too late, and lose a vital form of support on which successful schoolwide change depends.
Leadership	Leaders are either too controlling, too ineffectual, or cash in on the early success of the innovation to move on to higher things.
Relationship to Other Initiatives	The change is pursued in isolation and gets undermined by other unchanged structures. Conversely, the change may be poorly coordinated with and engulfed by a tidal wave of parallel changes that make it hard for teachers to focus their effort.

[1]Synthesized from Hargreaves (1997a), pp. viii.

The Nature of Inclusive Schools

What type of changes make a school more inclusive? A lack of clarity about what inclusion means has led to a wide variety of responses to this question. In addressing this issue, it is helpful to consider what inclusion is, as well as what it is not.

Advocates of inclusive schooling practices are portrayed as zealots who "....place philosophy before the needs of children" (Smelter, Rasch & Yudewitz, 1994, pg. 38). A common theme among critics of inclusion is that general education placement of students with disabilities denies them the individualized, special education supports that they need, shifting the burden [sic] for educating these students to unprepared general educators. Examples of these perspectives, drawn from both the special and general education literature, are contained in Table 2. Kauffman and Hallahan summarize this view in their description of the inclusion bandwagon (1995):

> *The full inclusion bandwagon offers an attractive platform - the merger of special and general education into a seamless and supple system that will support all students adequately in general schools and general education classrooms, regardless of any student's characteristics. Those offering cautions warn that this platform, although having an appealing sheen, is not sufficiently substantial for students who make particularly heavy demands on any system of education* (pg. ix).

It is clear that many unsound educational practices surrounding the placement of students with disabilities in general education settings are erroneously characterized as "inclusion". Lipsky and Gartner's (1996) definition of inclusion is representative of those offered by advocates of this practice, clearly speaking to the provision of specialized supports within general education settings.

> **Inclusion** [emphasis added] *is the provision of services to students with disabilities, including those with severe impairments, in the neighborhood school, in age-appropriate general education classes, with the necessary support services and supplementary aids (for the child and the teacher) both to assure the child's success - academic, behavioral and social - and to prepare the child to participate as a full and contributing member of the society* (Lipsky & Gartner, 1996, pg. 763).

Table 2
Common Misperceptions About Inclusion

Misperception	Examples from the Educational Literature
inclusion is dumping	Most of the 5 million children with disabilities now in public schools are described as being "included", meaning they spend their days in regular classrooms. But we found that *"inclusion," once called "mainstreaming", often results in dumping* [emphasis added]. Too often the classroom teacher has no special training and little additional support (Merrow, 1996, pg. 48). We use the related term "full inclusion" to refer to the practice of having regular education teachers teach both regular education students and special education students together, *without the assistance of a special education teacher* [emphasis added] (Smelter, Rasch & Yudewitz, 1994, pg. 36).
inclusion means that students with disabilities will not receive special education or specialized instruction	...providing the same curriculum and instructional methods used with children free of disabilities for children with different learning needs is patently unfair (MacMillan, Gresham, & Forness, 1996, pg. 148). One essential difficulty of the full inclusion philosophy is that it presumes that the children with learning disabilities or with mental retardation would be studying the same curriculum as the average student - but perhaps at a slower pace (Gallagher, 1995, pg. 99). The "inclusive school" denotes a place rid of special educators, where full inclusion reigns (Fuchs & Fuchs, 1994, pg. 299).
inclusion means full time placement in general education for every minute of the instructional day	The current placement battle rages over full inclusion versus the individualization placement decision-making process required by law (Bateman, 1995, pg. 86). The inclusionist movement requires no close examination of the learning styles of individual children or of the settings in which they learn best. It also renders much of what takes place at the multidisciplinary staffing for special education placement a foregone conclusion. .... One has to make no individual case to parents; one merely recites a bundle of philosophical postulates. One can never be accused of "calling the shots wrong," for there are no "shots" to call (Smelter, Rasch & Yudewitz, 1994, pg. 38).

When the word inclusion is used as an adjective to describe a school, the definition broadens beyond a description of the delivery of special education supports

> *An* **inclusive school** [emphasis added] *is a place where everyone belongs, is accepted, supports, and is supported by his or her peers and other members of the school community in the course of having his or her educational needs met* (Stainback & Stainback, 1990, pg. 3).

Thus, **inclusive schooling practices** are those that lead to the creation of supportive educational communities in which services necessary to meet the individual needs of all students are available. This includes services previously available only in specialized settings. From this perspective, the interests, goals, and concerns of those advocating for inclusion are identical to those of general education reformers who seek to develop more responsive school communities (e.g., Sergiovanni, 1994). Specific strategies that support the creation of inclusive school communities, grounded in the literature about educational change, are examined in the next section.

Applying Lessons About Change to Inclusion

In a recent commentary, Eric Schaps (1997) expressed frustration about the current climate of reform, arguing that those who hold holistic, learner-centered visions of education are being overshadowed by those whose primary focus is quick fixes to achieve high levels of academic performance.

> *Those of us who believe worthwhile change is inescapably local, slow, and difficult have been shouldered out of the national debate. We have been pushed aside in favor of solutions that are simplistic, naive, and sometimes arrogant* (pg. 20).

He suggests that it is critical for those with diverse views and expectations about education to identify common ground - educational goals that have a broad base of support. For example, "most of us want schools to be both challenging and caring for the full range of students they serve" (Schaps, 1997, pg. 20).

A school in which all can learn and are valued is the vision of those who advocate for the inclusion of students with disabilities. In order to effectively work toward these goals, lessons derived from the study of educational change must be considered. In Table 3, the impediments to change described by Hargreaves (1997a) are once again identified (see Table 1 for definitions). For each of these areas, proactive strategies to avoid these potential pitfalls are suggested.

Table 3
Strategies to Facilitate Inclusion Derived from the Change Literature

Consideration	Implications to Facilitate Inclusion
Rationale	The rationale for inclusion must be developed in collaboration with general educators and communicated in terms relative to the needs and benefits of all students. Inclusion must be a professional value that encompasses ALL students. Support and acceptance of student diversity must be a common goal. Anticipated benefits to non-special education students should be emphasized.
Scope	Inclusion is a fundamental change, but the inclusion of students with disabilities is often initiated incrementally, beginning with one or two students. Support issues are resolved with these students to demonstrate positive outcomes and gain full school support. Unless this initial effort addresses existing structures, roles, and resources, these small steps are not likely to lead to larger scale change.
Pace	The pace of change must fit the setting. Placing all students with disabilities in general education classes too rapidly will leave staff unclear about their new roles and expectations. In contrast, moving too slowly can lead to criticism about the lack of visible outcomes. Collaborative planning is necessary to set and review the pace, accelerating it or decelerating it to fit the setting.
Resources	The move to inclusion must be supported with resources to gain full team commitment. Resources in the form of release time, technical assistance time, and substitute time are especially important to assure adequate planning. Inclusion should not mean a decrease in special education or related services supports. It does mean that resources are used differently, including in different locations. Dedicated and creative teams can find and develop resources others might not recognize.
Commitment	The commitment to inclusive schooling practices must be broad-based. This is not just a special education initiative; efforts require the entire school facility. Planning, rationale, scope, pace, and resources must be developed through the collaboration of a broad spectrum of school personnel and families.
Key Staff	The impetus to include students with disabilities often originates with special educators. This can lead to a situation where inclusion is viewed a single person's "project". Collaborative teaming, involving administrators, families, students, general educators, and special educators, must be recognized as necessary and supported components of successful inclusion. Key staff from all areas of the school must be involved in the implementation of this innovation.
Parents	Parents of both general and special education students should be involved in discussions and planning about inclusion so that misunderstandings are minimized and concerns are addressed from the beginning.

Consideration	Implications to Facilitate Inclusion
Leadership	Administrative support and leadership are crucial for school wide adoption of inclusion. Successful leaders recognize the power of team collaboration, and use these structures to guide the implementation of inclusive schooling practices.
Relationship to Other Initiatives	Inclusion fits well with many current educational initiatives to improve the learning outcomes for all students. Rather than being viewed as a separate initiative, issues relative to students with disabilities should be considered within the context of the other instructional and organizational agendas of the school.

With these strategies for promoting change as a starting point, the next issue to consider is what specific practices need to be changed. Viable approaches for accommodating the needs of diverse students are described in the following section, providing a full array of potential change targets for schools seeking to become more inclusive.

Part II:
Educational Structures and Practices that Support Diversity

Differences hold great opportunities for learning. Differences offer a free, abundant, and renewable resource. I would like to see our compulsion for eliminating differences replaced by an equally compelling focus on making use of these differences to improve schools. What is important about people - and about schools - is what is different, not what is the same (Barth, 1990, pp. 514-515)

For many years, general and special educators have been concerned with accommodating the needs of diverse learners in the general education classroom. As the number of students with disabilities in general education settings increases (Katsiyannis et al., 1995; U.S Department of Education, 1996), debate about this issue continues in the professional literature, school buildings, board rooms, and courtrooms. While these discussions are an inevitable part of the change process, they divert attention from the issues that directly impact the ability of educators to create educationally responsive environments. The fundamental practices and characteristics of our schools - the prevailing curriculum and instructional strategies as well as the roles, skills, and attitudes of teachers - must be examined as students with varying abilities are placed in general education classrooms.

In this section, issues of curriculum, instruction, and school organization are considered from the vantage point of practices that support and honor the full range of learners in a school. First, a broad context of "best instructional practice" is established, synthesizing current thinking about how to reach all learners. This is followed by a discussion of school culture and climate characteristics associated with these instructional practices. Finally, organizational structures that support the approaches discussed are considered.

Responsive Instructional Practices

Curricular reform initiatives have been fueled by dissatisfaction among multiple constituencies, from those who feel that the most capable students are not adequately challenged, to those concerned about less advantaged students, who too often do not succeed in a curriculum that "ignores their background, minimizes their motivation for academic work, and prepares them neither for advanced education nor for the technological demands of new vocational options" (Pugach & Warger, 1996a, pg. 2). Cuban (1989) describes schools as lacking the flexibility to accommodate the diverse abilities and interests of a heterogeneous student body. Current discussions about educational best practice, grounded in the need to create more responsive learning environments, draw upon what is known about how students learn. Major themes that characterize these discussions are identified below, with examples of instructional methods that reflect these recommended best practices.

■   *Integrated approaches to curricular content promote learning* (e.g., Dewey, 1938, 1943; Monda-Amaya & Pearson, 1996).

Despite a long history of prominent voices advocating for integrated, child-centered approaches to teaching (e.g., Dewey, 1938, 1943), the tradition of separate, specialized subjects is a strong and continuing force in American education. Monda-Amaya and Pearson (1996) argue that integrated instructional approaches are likely to be: (a) more interconnected and less intimidating to students; (b) more relevant and motivating to students; and (c) potentially more efficient, since they reduce instructional duplication. Teachers involved in creating an integrated science program, for example, describe their efforts as resulting in "engaging experiences in which students encounter essential content in multiple and meaningful contexts in response to their own inquiry" (Eggebrecht, Dagenais, Dosch, Merczak, Park, Styer & Workman, 1996, pg. 5).

At the elementary level, thematic units have been the most popular means of achieving curricular integration. At the secondary level, integrated instruction may refer to integration across subject areas or integration within a single, broad discipline such as science (e.g., Koba, 1996; Prescott, Rinard, Cockerill & Baker, 1996). A critical characteristic of this approach is framing instruction around real situations and problems (e.g., Alper, Fendel, Fraser & Resek, 1996).

■   *Thinking and intelligence are not singular constructs. Instruction should be delivered in a way that capitalizes upon different ways of learning* (Dunn, 1996; Gardner, 1983; Sternberg, 1994).

The growing popularity of Howard Gardner's theory of multiple intelligences has stimulated interest in multi-modal approaches to teaching. While the traditional classroom relies heavily upon linguistic and logical-mathematical skills, multiple intelligences theory encourages teachers to develop curricula and plan their lessons in ways that build upon other forms of learning and expression. The Key School in Indianapolis, reorganized to create a total learning experience for students (Bolanos, 1990), illustrates that successful restructuring around this concept can occur. The Key School's philosophy is that all children should be provided with an equitable education. Students previously labeled as "learning disabled" and "gifted" are placed within heterogeneous classrooms. The wide range of abilities within the classroom is a factor seen as enriching the program (Armstrong, 1994). Curricular experiences address the entire spectrum of intelligences, offering instruction in music, dance, visual arts, computers, and foreign language as well as the basic subjects.

The work of Sternberg and his colleagues (Sternberg, 1994; Sternberg & Spear-Swerling, 1996) represents another model that explicitly identifies and emphasizes the variety of abilities present, to varying degrees, in all learners. He speaks of memory, analysis, creativity, and practicality as four distinct learning abilities. In a study of 200 students designed to test the hypothesis that students learn and perform better when they are taught in a way that at least partially matches their learning strengths, results indicated that students whose instruction matched their pattern of abilities performed significantly better than those whose instruction was not matched in this way (Sternberg, 1997).

A third prominent framework for thinking about differences in the process of learning speaks of learning *style*. As illustrated in Table 4 there are models that describe style differences in terms of cognition, conceptualization, and affective behavior. Again, there is evidence to suggest that instruction matched to a student's preferred style is associated with positive performance gains (e.g., Dunn, Griggs, Olson, Gorman & Beasley, 1995; Hodgin & Wooliscroft, 1997).

Table 4
Models that Describe Differences in Learning Style[1]

Behavior	Range of Traits	Theorist/Researcher
Cognition - how a student perceives, finds out, and gets information	◆ sending→intuition	Jung (1971); Myers-Briggs (1962); Mok (1975); Keirsey & Bates (1978)
	◆ field dependent→ field independent	Witkin et al. (1977)
	◆ abstract→concrete	Gregorc (1982); Kolb (1976); McCarthy (1980)
	◆ visual, auditory, kinesthetic, tactile	Barbe & Swassing (1979); Dunn & Dunn (1975)
Conceptualization - how a student thinks, forms ideas, processes information, and remembers	◆ extravert→introvert	Jung (1971); Myers-Briggs (1962); Keirsey &Bates (1978)
	◆ reflective observation→active experimentation	Kolb (1976); McCarthy (1980)
	◆ random→sequential	Gregorc (1982)
Affect - the feelings, types of emotional responses, motivation, values, and judgements that characterize a learner	◆ feeler→thinker	Jung (1971); Myers-Briggs (1962); Mok (1975); Keisey & Bates (1978)
	◆ effect of temperature, light, food, time of day, sound, design	Dunn & Dunn (1975)

[1]Adapted from Guild & Garger (1985).

■   ***Teaching for thinking, problem solving, and understanding has positive
    effects on student achievement (Newmann & Wehlage, 1993).***

A variety of non-traditional approaches to teaching, sharing theoretical origins
in the work of Dewey, Piaget, Bruner, and Vygotsky, are predominant in current
discussions and projects demonstrating effective instructional practice. Examples
include "teaching for understanding" (Perkins & Blythe, 1994), constructivist learning
(Brookes & Brookes, 1993), authentic instruction (Newmann & Wehlage, 1993),
accelerated schools (Hopfenberg & Levin, 1993), and problem-based learning
(Stepien & Gallagher, 1993). These approaches share several characteristics:

   ◆   an emphasis on developing understanding through doing;
   ◆   instructional supports for extending student knowledge by
          building upon what they already know; and
   ◆   increasing student involvement in and responsibility for what
          they learn.

Rather than the traditional "teacher transmission" approach to instruction,
educators grounded in this philosophy function as facilitators and mediators of student
learning. Teachers use questioning as a tool to stimulate thinking and exploration,
guiding students through exploration and discovery. Students frequently work in
small groups on activities that rely heavily on primary sources of data and
manipulative materials. Translating constructivist thinking into instructional practice
calls into question most aspects of the traditional school structure. For example,
classrooms that are dominated by teacher talk (Goodland, 1984), rely upon textbooks
as the primary source of information (Ben-Peretz, 1990), and use predominantly
individualistic or competitive task structures (Johnson & Johnson, 1991) do not
promote constructivist learning in students.

■   ***Assessment should be integrally connected to learning and teaching***
    (Danielson, 1995; Darling-Hammond, Ancess & Falk, 1995).

In the educational context described above, traditional approaches to
measuring student growth are incongruent with basic beliefs about teaching and
learning. True-false, multiple choice, and other common approaches to testing focus
on knowledge of discrete skills, failing to capture what students are able to do with
information in situations that require higher order thinking and problem solving. The
term *authentic assessment* refers to evaluation activities that "actively involve students
in a process that joins what is taught, how it is taught, and how it is evaluated"
(Kreisman, Knoll & Melchior, 1995, pg. 114). Information-gathering about student
learning is accomplished through observation, interviews, questionnaires, checklists,
student artifacts, work samples, performance assessment, student self-evaluation,
evaluation conferences, portfolios, and other tools that provide students an opportunity
to demonstrate and explain their progress.

Zemelman and colleagues (1993) identified best practice guidelines for student evaluation. They include the following:

♦ recognize that the purpose of most assessment is formative, not summative; involve students in record-keeping and in judging their own work;

♦ teachers triangulate their assessments, looking at each child from several angles, by drawing on observation, conversation, artifacts, performances, etc;.

♦ evaluation activities are part of instruction (such as in teacher-student conferences), rather than separate from it;

♦ teachers spend a moderate amount of their time on evaluation and assessment, not allowing it to rule their professional lives or consume their instruction; and

♦ where possible, competitive grading systems are abolished or de-emphasized (Zemelman et al., 1993).

Strategies to Accommodate Specific Barriers to Learning

The previous section highlighted basic premises that underlie instructional practices intended to be responsive to the different ways students learn. Other strategies, drawn largely from the support repertoire of special educators and psychologists, provide options for accommodations and modifications that enable students with substantial learning differences to participate and benefit from general education classroom instruction. The themes that capture the range and intent of these supports are highlighted below.

■ *Some students require explicit instruction about "how to learn" in the general education classroom* (Schumaker, Deshler & Ellis, 1986).

Deshler, Schumaker and their colleagues at the University of Kansas Institute for Research in Learning Disabilities are prominent among special educators who have designed approaches to teach students with disabilities *how* to learn in the general education classroom. The focus of their Strategies Intervention Model is to teach skills that enable students to successfully analyze and solve novel problems encountered in academic and nonacademic environments (Deshler & Schumaker, 1986). They have developed strategies to help students acquire information from written materials, identify and store important information, and facilitate written expression and demonstration of competence. The structure and demands of a particular general education setting determine which strategies are emphasized, leading to greater student success in the general education classroom.

All of the specific strategies that are a part of this model have been systematically evaluated as part of a research and development process (e.g., Clark, Deshler, Schumaker & Alley, 1984; Schumaker, Deshler, Alley & Warner, 1983). In each case, a vast majority of the students involved in instruction have been successfully taught to use the strategy, and have realized academic gains as a result of its use (Deshler & Schumaker, 1986).

■   ***An array of strategies have been developed that enable students to learn the general education curriculum*** (e.g., Choate, 1993; Edwards, 1980; Johnson & Johnson, 1980; Turnbull & Schultz, 1979).

There is a substantial body of literature focused on the modification of curriculum materials to support students with disabilities who are mainstreamed into general education classrooms.   These approaches primarily rely upon the general education teacher to make adjustments in his/her instruction based upon recommendations provided by a special educator.   Instruction can be adapted by changing one or more dimensions of the lesson, including:

♦   the way in which instruction is delivered;
♦   the amount of content covered;
♦   the criteria used to evaluate student performance;
♦   the level of assistance provided to the student;
♦   the learning environment; and/or
♦   the instructional materials used by the student (Beninghof & Singer, 1995).

While a wide variety of options are available for adapting the learning environment to meet the needs of an individual student, the frame of reference in many classrooms continues to be the standard curriculum. If a student cannot reasonably be expected to succeed relative to the standards established for the "typical" students with supports, that triggers the   student's removal from the classroom for more specialized instruction (Schultz, Carpenter & Turnbull, 1991). This is the point at which mainstreaming models and more recently developed inclusive schooling practices depart.

■   ***Concepts of curricular modification and accommodation have broadened as students with more severe disabilities have become valued members of general education classrooms*** (e.g., Giangreco, Cloninger & Iverson, 1993; Heron & Jorgensen, 1995; Udvari-Solner, 1995).

Current perspectives on curricular adaptation do not presume that students with disabilities will always be working on the same or similar goals in the same curricular area as their typical peers. *Curriculum overlapping* has been developed as a viable strategy for considering regular classroom participation of students with widely differing abilities and educational needs. This approach occurs when "a diverse group of students is involved in the same lesson, but they are pursuing goals and objectives from different curricular areas" (Giangreco et al., 1993, pg. 23). Thus, the regular classroom activity is used as a vehicle to teach students goals that are important for them. This option for participation eliminates the need to exclude students simply because they are unable to perform at the same level as their peers.

■   *Planning for the full range of learners at the design point of instruction minimizes the amount of "retrofitting" that must be provided by special education personnel working to support students in the general education classroom* (Udvari-Solner, 1995).

A second conceptual difference in current perspectives about curricular modifications concerns the point at which special educators become involved in curricular planning and decision-making. In mainstreaming models, specialists design modifications that support the learning of students with disabilities within the context of the general educator's lesson plans. In this model, a key concern is the "do-ability" of the accommodation from the perspective of the general educator (Schumm & Vaughn, 1991). More recent approaches bring special and general educators together at the initial planning stages of a lesson. When this occurs, it is far more likely that adaptive teaching methods will be "frontloaded" (Heron & Jorgensen, 1994), rather than added after-the-fact by a special educator who may or may not have time to communicate alternative performance plans to the general education teacher before the lesson is delivered.

Creating Caring and Supportive Learning Communities

A community of learners is an educational setting in which children are encouraged to care about each other and about their learning. Sergiovanni defines community as...

> *the tie that binds students and teachers together in special ways, to something more significant than themselves: shared values and ideals.... Community can help teachers and students be transformed from a collection of "I's" to a collective "we", thus providing them with a unique and enduring sense of identity, belonging and place* (1994, pg. xiii).

Consistent recommendations emerge from the literature that address the creation of such supportive environments in classrooms and schools. The predominant themes derived from these discussions are identified and briefly described below.

■   ***In caring communities, an appreciation of differences is fostered through a curriculum that emphasizes friendship, caring, and a respect for diversity*** (Child Development Project, 1994; Dalton & Watson, 1997; Kohn, 1991).

Addressing a group of teachers in 1939, Martin Buber stated, "Education worthy of the name is essentially education of character (Buber/Smith, 1965, p. 104). His message was that teaching should involve stimulating not merely good learners, but also students that are good people (Kohn, 1991). The struggle to articulate and clarify the role of schools in this area continues to this day, at times seemingly lost in emotionally charged debates about religion, values, and the purpose of education. The easiest solution for schools is to simply not address these issues in the curriculum, sticking to the safer ground of academics. However, students learn much from what Ryan (1993) terms "the hidden curriculum".

Many of education's most profound and positive teachings can be conveyed in the hidden curriculum. If a spirit of fairness penetrates every corner of a school, children will learn to be fair...While unseen, the hidden curriculum must be considered with the same seriousness as the written, formal curriculum (pg. 18).

Reflective teachers such as Vivian Paley (1992) have explored classroom strategies and expectations (e.g., "you can't say you can't play) to reduce the occurrence of behaviors among children that lead to the oft expressed sentiment "kids can be cruel!". Transforming Paley's philosophy and book title into a qualitative study, Sapon-Shevin and four teacher/researchers sought to find out whether teachers can influence children's interactions by implementing a classroom rule that supports the inclusion of all (Sapon-Shevin, Dobbelaere, Cirrigan, Goodman & Mastin, 1998). While not a cure-all in itself, the rule was viewed as a powerful organizing principle in each of these classrooms, contributing to a rich discourse about inclusion issues. The teachers describe the use of journals, role play, problem solving, and class meetings in their efforts to make the rule a part of the daily life of their classrooms.

On a broader scale, attention to social and ethical dimensions of learning is a cornerstone of schools adopting practices advocated by the Child Development Project, a comprehensive school-change effort focused on helping elementary schools become inclusive, caring, and stimulating learning communities (Child Development Project, 1994). In such schools, five essential ingredients, highlighted in Table 5, are emphasized to create a sense of community within the school. Results of this project indicate that students work hard, achieve more, and attribute more importance to schoolwork in classes in which they feel liked, accepted, and respected by the teacher and fellow students (Lewis, Schaps & Watson, 1996).

■   ***Cooperative structures promote the value of learning together and helping others*** (Johnson & Johnson, 1991, 1989; Kohn, 1992; Nicholls, 1989).

Within individual classrooms, collaboration is fostered through the use of small group structures. Motivated by the vision of collaborative learning reflected in the work of Glasser (1990), Johnson and Johnson (e.g., 1991), Slavin (Slavin et al., 1985; Slavin, 1990) and others, many collaborative approaches to learning are routinely being used in general education classrooms. Approaches such as those highlighted in Table 6 encourage students to be actively involved in their learning with peers.

Table 5
Child Development Project's Essential Ingredients to Promote Community-Building[2]

Inclusion and Participation	Emphasis on Helping Others and Taking Responsibility
◆ All parents, children, and school staff members are invited to participate freely in schoolwide activities, particularly those designed for families to enjoy together.	◆ Children are given the opportunity to experience the value of helping others.
◆ Invitations are warm, welcoming, and nonthreatening.	◆ Everyone takes responsibility within and outside the school community.
◆ Activities are designed with attention to special language, cultural, economic, and child care needs of participating families.	**Appreciation of Differences**
Cooperative Environment	◆ Parents, children, and school staff members feel that their social and cultural backgrounds are valued and respected within the school community.
◆ Children and families are able to enjoy cooperative, noncompetitive activities that promote the value of learning together and helping others.	◆ Everyone is encouraged to share his or her cultural heritage and learn from others.
◆ Everyone succeeds at learning; there are no losers.	**Reflection**
	◆ Everyone is encouraged to reflect on what has been learned from the experience of working together.

[2] (CDP, 1994, pg. 12).

Table 6
Small Group Structures that Encourage Collaboration in Heterogeneous Groups

Description of Approach	Application of Practice with Diverse Groups
partner/buddy reading (Zemelman et al., 1993)	Two students take turns reading aloud to each other from a story or textbook. Ability differences can be accommodated by individualizing the reading material.
peer response and editing (Zemelman et al., 1993)	Students read and provide feedback to each other on drafts of their work. Use of computer-based spelling and grammar checks can assist students edit work that they might not be able to produce. Similarly, students can provide feedback about the clarity of writing when the author reads the material to them.

Description of Approach	Application of Practice with Diverse Groups
literature circles/text sets (Zemelman et al., 1993)	Groups of four or five students choose and read the same article or book. They come to the literature circle with an assigned discussion role. Careful role assignment can accommodate skill differences, as can different versions and modalities (tape, film) of the same book.
study teams (DeVries, Slavin, Fennessey, Edwards & Lombardo, 1980)	Useful when students must memorize facts, heterogeneous learning teams are established in which students are encouraged to ensure that all members learn the materials through a reward system based on the performance of the entire group. Within teams, it is possible to establish individual expectations, and reward can be structured on each person in the group achieving their own goal.
learning together (Johnson & Johnson, 1991)	Students are divided into heterogeneous groups of two to six, and provided with one set of learning materials. Emphasis in on sharing and support among group members. Mastery of material is measured by individual test/grades or group products.
group investigations (Kagan, 1985; Sharan & Hertz-Lazarowitz, 1980)	Often introduced during a whole class discussion, a problem for study is identified. Information, hypotheses, and questions are raised; groups of students are formed based on their interest and skill in investigating some facet of the problem. The team reconvenes to share and discuss their findings.
jigsaw (Aronson et al., 1978)	Students are placed in heterogeneous groups and assigned one section/component of a topic. They are then responsible for investigating that topic and sharing information learned with other group members. They meet with students from other groups (expert groups) who were assigned the same topic to exchange information and master the material that they will present to their own group members. Different abilities and interest can be taken into account in the assignment of topics and the composition of "expert" groups.
think-pair-share (Lyman, 1992)	Temporary pairing of students with partners to share ideas and develop responses to a question posed to the entire class. This procedure ensure that every student would have a response to share with the class based on their discussion with a partner.
numbered heads together (Kagan, 1985)	This strategy is designed to actively engage all students during adult-led instruction and discussion. Students are organized into four-member heterogeneous learning teams. After the teacher directs a question to the entire class, students are asked to "put their heads together" to come up with their best answer, and make sure all group members know the answer. The teacher then asks for answers from one numbered member of a group (e.g., "Which number 1 can answer this question?").

Elizabeth Cohen's (1994) research in the area of structuring small groups provides specific guidelines for selecting tasks that accommodate a wide range of intellectual abilities in small group activities. *Multiple abilities* tasks create a context in which all students can actively participate. As defined by Cohen, a multiple ability task:

- Has more than one answer or more than one way to solve the problem;
- Is intrinsically interesting and rewarding;
- Allows different students to make different contributions;
- Uses multimedia;
- Involves sight, sound, and touch;
- Requires a variety of skills and behaviors;
- Also requires reading and writing; and
- Is challenging (Cohen, 1994, pg. 68).

Beyond ensuring equitable participation through careful task structuring, cooperatively structured activities include active instruction in the social aspects of working together. It is this aspect of collaborative group structuring that is so clearly related to the creation of a supportive learning community. As outlined by Dalton and Watson (1997) and described in Table 7, collaborative learning groups provide a context in which many prosocial student behaviors can be taught and reinforced.

A substantial body of research confirms the academic and social benefits of collaborative approaches to instruction, including peer tutoring (Cohen, Kulik & Kulik, 1982) and cooperative learning, for students of diverse abilities. Benefits have been noted in measures of student achievement (e.g., Johnson & Johnson, 1989a,b; Johnson, Maruyama, Johnson, Nelson & Skon, 1981; Sharan, 1980; Slavin, 1990), affect and self esteem (e.g., Johnson & Johnson, 1989a; Wright & Cowen, 1985; Zahn, Kagan & Widaman, 1986) and peer relationships and interactions (e.g., Johnson & Johnson, 1984; Johnson, Johnson & Anderson, 1983; Johnson, Johnson & Maruyama, 1983; Johnson, Johnson, Warring & Maruyama, 1986; Madden & Slavin, 1983a,b).

Table 7
Collaborative Skills that Can Be Promoted Through Small Group Learning[3]

Fairness	Responsibility	Concern and Respect for Others	Helpfulness
Equal Participation ◆ asking questions to get everyone's ideas, opinions, & feelings ◆ taking turns ◆ letting everyone have a change to talk ◆ making sure everyone has a job or part of the task ◆ sharing materials **Fair Decision Making** ◆ getting all options before making a decision ◆ choosing a fair way to decide ◆ supporting the group's agreement or decision ◆ stating your ideas, opinions, and feelings	◆ asking questions to get a clear understanding ◆ asking others in your group for help when you need it ◆ putting forth extra effort when necessary ◆ letting others know when you disagree and why ◆ making sure you do your part of the work ◆ doing your best ◆ helping the group stay focused on the work ◆ following the ground rules for cooperative group work	◆ making suggestion without being bossy ◆ listening to the person who is talking ◆ encouraging differing opinions ◆ being sensitive to different abilities and needs ◆ disagreeing in a respectful way ◆ expressing appreciation and support for others' ideas and work	◆ checking to make sure others understand (the task, question, or answer) ◆ showing or explaining without doing the other person's work ◆ taking a part when someone has a job that is too big or too hard

[3]Dalton & Watson, 1997, pg. 47.

■   *Classroom practices that teach self-control, problem solving, and basic values reinforce a sense of community* (Apple & Beane, 1995; Charney, 1991, 1997).

Those who advocate for more democratic school structures argue that these contexts enable faculty and staff to view themselves as members of a learning community (Solomon, Schaps, Watson & Battistich, 1992). In order for students to be more active and self-directed learners, a context must be established in which teacher and students share responsibility for the learning environment. At the school and classroom level, students can be partners in the discussions and decision-making that ultimately shapes the daily practices of the school. An underlying commitment to equity and the common good creates a context in which differences present opportunities for discussion and problem-solving, rather than serving as a basis for separation. Research suggests that elementary-aged students have the skills and reasoning ability to enable them to engage in such democratic approaches to group decision-making (Turiel, 1987).

Collaborative problem-solving has been successfully used for the specific purpose of involving diverse learners in general education classrooms (e.g.,

Giangreco, Cloninger, Dennis & Edelman, 1995; Salisbury, Evans & Palombaro, 1997). In these classrooms, students successfully developed solutions for involving all students in classroom activities, dealing with staffing problems, responding to issues of social exclusion, and barriers to interaction posed by a student's physical limitations. Beyond resolving immediate problems, researchers documented an increased concern for others, acceptance of diversity, and empowerment to create change among students who were members of this class (Salisbury et al., 1997).

This same philosophy is evident in a growing number of alternative approaches to student management currently implemented in schools across the country. Disillusioned by traditional behavior management approaches based exclusively on external controls and contingencies, these approaches emphasize student responsibility and involvement in the resolution of conflict and problem behavior. (e.g., Lantieri & Patti, 1996; Porro, 1996; Schneider, 1996).

■ *Linking instruction to real situations expands the concept of classroom, curriculum, and community* (e.g., Christ, 1995; Thompson, 1995).

Goodlad's (1984) concept of the "educative community" is reflected in innovative curricular approaches that expand the concept of the school building as the primary place for learning. In his view, the entire environment must educate, and everyone within this environment must become both educator and learner. Service learning projects (Curwin, 1993; Howard, 1993) exemplify this expanded view of classroom and curriculum, providing students with real-world experiences and opportunities to make real contributions to their school and community through experiences that are matched with their individual interests and strengths.

Problem-based learning is another instructional approach that often actively links the school with the larger community. With roots in the experiences of medical educators (Aspy, Aspy & Quinby, 1993), classroom teachers are discovering the value of problem-based approaches to learning for stimulating student interest and strengthening student involvement in the issues and concerns of their home communities (Burke, 1993). A third example of integrating community outreach into the curriculum is the study of "ordinary heros" (Reissman, 1995). Useful as a mechanism to engage students in connecting with the resources of their own community, it also provides rich opportunities to explore the values that define a hero.

Organizational Structures that Support Responsive Schooling Practices

The structures that define the use of time, space, and personnel provide a foundation for the curricular practices of a school. In this section, organizational themes that capture approaches that readily support the instructional practices previously described are highlighted.

■   *Meaningful, integrated approaches to instruction require alternative approaches to highly segmented school day schedules* (Zemelman et al., 1993).

The schedule is a critical school resource. As described by Canady and Rettig (1995), a schedule can help solve problems related to the delivery of instruction as well as facilitate the institutionalization of desired programs and instructional practices.

Scheduling practices at the elementary level make it possible for individual teachers to adopt instructional innovations such as curriculum integration. Since these classrooms are typically self-contained, teachers have the freedom to organize time within their own classroom. Involvement with other teachers or specialists, however, can be limited if schedules do not provide opportunities to plan and work together. In traditional middle and high schools, there is much less flexibility in the schedule to support such instructional practices. Critics of the traditional seven to eight period schedule characterize this model as a design for incoherence (Zemelman et al., 1993) for both teachers and students.

Alternative approaches to scheduling that produce extended time blocks for learning (i.e., block schedules) are increasingly being adopted by schools to support a variety of reform initiatives. In a national study of high school restructuring, Cawelti (1994) found that 38% of the schools responding to this survey indicated that block scheduling was used to some extent or was being planned for the next school year. Many approaches to block scheduling have emerged. Table 8 provides a description of common designs that have emerged during the 1990's.

Calwelti (1994) identified the potential benefits of block schedules to include:

◆   increased length of class periods;
◆   enables teachers to use a variety of instructional approaches;
◆   decreases the number of class changes;
◆   saves time;
◆   limits the number of preparations for individual teachers;
◆   provides the opportunity for interdisciplinary teaching;
◆   decreases the number of students taught each day by a teacher;
◆   increases planning time for teachers;
◆   helps teachers to develop closer relationships with their students;
◆   provides the opportunity for project work; and
◆   provides additional opportunities for teachers to help students.

Table 8
Block Scheduling Models[4]

Model	Description of Practice
alternative day plan or "slide" schedule	Classes meet every other day, rather than daily, for extended time blocks or at different times during the day on a rotating basis
"4 by 4" or accelerated plan	Students enroll in four courses which meet for approximately 90 minutes every day; courses are completed in a semester rather than a full year
trimester, quarter-on-quarter-off, and other intensive scheduling models	Other forms of providing instructional courses in more intensive time periods (e.g., 60 day periods)
reconfigurations of the 180-day school year	Divisions of the 180 day school year into instructional periods of variable length (e.g., fall term = 75 days; middle term = 15 days; spring term = 75 days; end term = 15 days)

[4]Canady & Rettig, 1995

■ *Heterogeneous student grouping practices have distinct instructional advantages, and avoid the pedagogical, moral, and ethical problems associated with tracking* (Oakes, Wells, Yonezawa & Ray, 1997; Pool & Page, 1995; Wheelock, 1992).

Grouping students by ability continues to be the keystone structure of many schools in this country, despite a substantial body of evidence of its harmful effects for all but the most academically talented students (e.g., Dawson, 1987; Gamoran, 1992). In classrooms organized in the manner described below, it is easy to understand why many teachers strongly defend ability-grouped classes.

> *...the teacher is the center: she or he tells, presents, explains, and gives assignments. When they are not listening to the teacher and taking notes, students work quietly and individually at their desks, writing answers to questions about what the teacher has presented. The teacher is a pitcher of knowledge; students are vessels being filled up. For students, the day is filled mostly with transforming what they have heard into short written repetitions: blanks filled in, bubbles darkened, and rarely, sentences or paragraphs composed* (Zemelman, 1993, pg. 192-193).

In this context, good students work quietly, follow the rules, and listen to the teacher. It is expedient to separate students who don't learn well with this approach so that other students are not disrupted. Until teachers let go of the premise that all students learn in the same way (and therefore can be taught in the same way) and should perform at the same level, diversity will continue to be viewed as a threat to the integrity of the general education classroom.

The drawbacks of tracking have been extensively documented. Pool and Page (1995) summarize these outcomes as follows:

Tracking promotes "dumbed-down", skill-drill, ditto-drive, application-deficient curricula. It contributes to the destruction of student dreams and the production of low student self-esteem. Even when it is not intended, whole-class stratified grouping promotes elitism, de facto racism, and classism. These placements can start as early as six weeks into kindergarten; and even though placements supposedly are flexible, they generally are permanent (pg. 1).

In a three year longitudinal case study of ten secondary schools engaged in detracking, the practice of tracking came to be viewed as a major impediment to the instructional and curricular changes necessary to help all students achieve, stimulating the adoption of practices more supportive of diverse learners. As described by Oakes and Wells (1996):

...some teachers adopted new classroom strategies that they believed permitted students to show their abilities in previously unrecognized ways. For instance, teachers tried to couple project-based science and interactive math curricula, and they relied less on textbooks and more on cooperative small group learning. These changes helped teachers teach and appreciate students whose abilities differed from those traditionally lauded as superior students (pg. 304).

The lesson they have learned from their work in this area is that the culture of detracking is more important than the specific alternative or implementation strategy chosen to replace ability grouping (Oakes & Lipton, 1992).

■   ***The logic of heterogeneity extends to cross-grade grouping practices***
(Anderson & Pavan, 1993).

Another longstanding assumption in education is that students of the same age have similar learning needs and abilities. An alternative perspective underlies the practice of multi-age grouping, a growing practice in this country. Kasten and Clark (1993) define multi-age grouping as:

...any deliberate grouping of children that includes more than one traditional grade level in a single classroom community (pg. 3).

These classrooms are heterogeneous groups of students that are expected and encouraged to learn at their own rate. This requires a classroom environment that is flexible, and structured to accommodate learners who are at very different places. In multiage classrooms, students tend to remain with the same teacher for at least two years, reducing the loss of instructional time associated with grade to grade transitions (Udvari-Solner & Thousand, 1996).

The philosophy of nongradedness centers on the belief that individuals are unique and need different treatments to reach their maximum growth potential. The theories that underlie the practice of nongradedness are based upon research findings in the area of ability grouping, tracking (already discussed), and retention/promotion. Anderson and Pavan (1993) summarize the research conducted since 1909 on the issue of retention and promotion. The data overwhelmingly support the conclusion that holding students back has negative affects on academic achievement, personal adjustment, self-concept, and attitude toward school. Holmes and Matthews (1984) conclude:

Those who continue to retain pupils at grade level do so despite cumulative research evidence showing that the potential for negative effects consistently outweighs positive outcomes. Because this cumulative research evidence consistently points to negative effects of nonpromotion, the burden of proof legitimately falls on proponents of retention plans to show there is compelling logic indicating success of their plans when so many other plans have failed (pg. 232).

Research directly examining the practices of nongraded, multigraded, and ungraded grouping support the viability of this organizational approach (Anderson & Pavan, 1993). An early synthesis of studies comparing nongraded and graded elementary schools, encompassing research published between 1968 and 1971 (Pavan, 1973), reported more positive academic and mental health outcomes for students in nongraded schools. An update of that analysis (Anderson & Pavan, 1993) that includes 64 studies published between 1968 and 1990 favors nongraded schools on these same measures. Seventeen of these studies had a longitudinal focus. Results suggest that the longer students are in a nongraded school, the more likely it is that good things will happen to them both academically and attitudinally.

■ ***Time for teaming and reflection is critical to enable collaborative approaches to instruction to occur and continue to develop*** (Adelman & Walking-Eagle, 1997; NEA, 1994; Raywid, 1993).

Adelman and Walking-Eagle (1997) cite the words of an experienced teacher, capturing both the challenge and importance of organizational structures that build in collaborative time for teachers.

Identifying and finding time within the contracted school day to talk, to plan, to create, to be a lifelong learner, and to teach gnaws at me constantly (pg. 92).

Instructional and curricular practices described thus far, designed to provide high quality instruction that is likely to meet the needs of diverse learners, are collaborative in nature. Interdisciplinary teams design integrated instructional units. Special educators, related services personnel, and other instructional specialists (e.g., Title I, bilingual education personnel) collaborate and team teach with general educators in order to provide supports to students within the general education classroom. Efforts to connect classroom learning with experiences within the larger community involve collaboration within as well as beyond the school walls. Finding time to engage in the necessary planning is critical. Equally important is time to reflect on the success of new initiatives, to enable a cycle of continuous progress to occur.

The solution to this problem is very contextually based. Many creative approaches have been devised by schools engaged in the process of school reform (Raywid, 1993). Table 9 depicts the clustering of these strategies into five different categories as described in a publication by the National Education Association (1994).

Table 9
Strategies to Find Time to Collaborate[5]

Strategy	Description of Approach
Freed-up time	Use of arrangements such as enlisting administrators to teach classes, authorizing teaching assistants and college interns to teach classes under the direction of a teacher, and teacher teaming in order to free other teachers from direct student supervision in order to engage in collaborative planning.
Restructured time	Formally altering the time frame of the traditional calendar Use of arrangements such as enlisting administrators to teach classes, authorizing teaching assistants and college interns to teach classes under the direction of a teacher, and teacher teaming in order to free teachers from direct student supervision in order to engage in planning., school, day, or teaching schedule to provide planning time.
Common time	Scheduling that provides common time to support restructuring programs, interdisciplinary teams, subject-area planning, grade-level planning and/or student-specific planning.

Strategy	Description of Approach
Better-used time	Using currently available time for meeting and professional development activities more effectively through advanced planning and other organizational strategies.
Purchased time	Hiring additional teachers.

[5] NEA, 1994, p. 17.

Summary

The strategies and structures described in this section are intended to result in positive learner outcomes for a full array students, caring and supportive learning environments, and responsive organizational structures. Drawn from the knowledge base of both general and special education, an effort has been made to bring together practices that support the philosophy and intended outcomes of inclusive learning environments. Best instructional practices are exemplified by approaches that help students connect and use knowledge, thinking creatively, and solve problems. These strategies require a flexible and supportive environment in which friendship, cooperation, caring, and respect for diversity is modeled through what is taught, as well as how teaching and learning occur. These practices challenge traditional classroom teaching practices by expanding learning opportunities and modalities to meet the needs of an increasingly diverse student population.

Collectively, these practices define what it means to be learner-centered. Kohn (1996) has compiled indicators of learner-centeredness, based on the physical characteristics and routine practices of a classroom. Described in Table 10, these indicators transform the theoretical and empirical perspectives highlighted in this section into a tangible form, serving as a tool for educators and parents to identify practices that are contributing to or detracting from efforts to create inclusive learning environments.

Table 10
Indicators of Learner-Centeredness[6]

Classroom Characteristic	Good Signs	Possible Reasons for Concern
furniture	◆ Chairs around tables to facilitate interaction ◆ Comfortable areas for working	◆ Desks in rows or chairs all facing forward

Classroom Characteristic	Good Signs	Possible Reasons for Concern
walls	◆ Covered with students' work ◆ Evidence of student collaboration ◆ Signs, exhibits, or lists created by students rather than teacher ◆ Information about, and mementos of, those who spend time together in this classroom	◆ Bare ◆ Decorated with commercial posters ◆ List of consequences for misbehavior ◆ List of rules created by an adult ◆ Sticker(or star) chart or other evidence that students are rewarded or ranked ◆ Students' work displayed but it is (a) suspiciously flawless, or (b) only "the best" students' work, or (c) virtually all alike
sounds	◆ Frequent hum of activity and ideas being exchanged	◆ Frequent periods of silence and/or teacher's voice the loudest or most often heard
location of teacher	◆ Typically working with students so that it takes a moment to find him or her	◆ Typically front and center
teacher's voice	◆ Respectful, genuine, warm	◆ Controlling and imperious ◆ Condescending and saccharine-sweet
students' reactions to visitor	◆ Welcoming; eager to explain or demonstrate what they're doing or to use visitor as a resource	◆ Either unresponsive or hoping to be distracted from what they're doing
class discussion	◆ Students often address one another directly ◆ Emphasis on thoughtful exploration of complicated issues ◆ Students ask questions at least as often as teacher does	◆ All exchanges involve (or directed by) teacher; students wait to be called on ◆ Emphasis on facts and right answers ◆ Students race to be first to answer teacher's "who can tell me?" queries
tasks	◆ Different activities take place simultaneously	◆ All students usually do the same thing

Classroom Characteristic	Good Signs	Possible Reasons for Concern
around the school	◆ Inviting atmosphere ◆ Students' work fills hallway walls ◆ Bathrooms in good condition ◆ Faculty lounge warm and comfortable ◆ Office staff welcoming toward visitors and students ◆ Students helping in lunchroom, library, and with other school functions	◆ Stark, institutional feel ◆ Award, trophies, and prizes displayed, suggesting emphasis on triumph rather than community

[6]Kohn, 1996, pg. 55.

The strategies and structures highlighted here require new ways of thinking about teacher roles, responsibilities, and schedules. Responsive schooling practices can only be realized through supportive administrative structures that provide a foundation that facilitates change and innovation. Collectively, these strategies and supports provide a context and reference point for considering the available empirical evidence about the processes and outcomes of inclusive schools, the focus of the next section of this document.

Part III:
Research About Inclusive Schooling Practices

In this section, a large body of research is synthesized for the purpose of deriving lessons to guide current and future efforts to create inclusive schools. No claims of absolute comprehensiveness are made (i.e., not every study that has ever been conducted about inclusive practices is referenced). However, a concerted effort has been made to sample the *range* of issues that have been investigated relative to inclusion. Therefore, research cited in this section was selected on the basis of its representative value in informing our thinking, planning, and strategies to make schools and classrooms more responsive to the needs of the full array of students (Cooper, 1989).

Unlike other recent reviews that have established strict contextual, participant, and/or methodological parameters to limit the body of research considered (e.g., Hunt & Goetz, 1997; Manset & Semmel, 1997), this synthesis takes a "wide net" approach, bringing together recent research as well as efforts implemented at a time when *mainstreaming* or the *integration* of students with disabilities was the predominant paradigm. The purpose of this approach is to capture the evolutionary quality of a continually growing knowledge base. Toward this end, an emphasis has been placed on identifying those studies that demonstrate successful outcomes. Collectively, strategies derived from these examples contribute to our knowledge of what is necessary to create general education classrooms in which all can be successful. Information from unsuccessful studies, however, can also inform, and has been used to identify unmet needs and contribute to the discussion of necessary supports and effective strategies. Due to the predominant role of advocates for students with severe disabilities in promoting and exploring approaches for successful inclusion (Fuchs & Fuchs, 1994), efforts focused on students with severe disabilities are strongly represented in this review. However, research focused on other populations is also referenced. Collectively, this begins to create a picture in which lessons extracted to guide future efforts are grounded in the richness of experience gained across time, in a variety of settings, and from multiple perspectives.

Perceptions of Key Stakeholders About Inclusion

Recent discussions about educational change emphasize the need to consider the emotional status of those critical to the success of an innovation (Hargreaves, 1997b). There is a large body of research that informs this perspective, consisting of descriptive studies that document the perceptions and feelings of key players involved in the movement toward more inclusive schooling practices. Information focused on each of these groups is summarized in this section.

Parent Perspectives

Much of the published information describing parent perspectives about the involvement of children with and without disabilities in school comes from the preschool and early education literature. Studies involving parents of young children with and without disabilities do not reveal major differences in perspectives about these programs (Reichart, Lynch, Anderson, Svobodny, DiCola & Mercury, 1989; Turnbull & Winton, 1983; Turnbull, Winton, Blacher & Salkind, 1982). Both groups of parents have been found to be largely supportive of inclusive approaches to education. Among the minority of parents of typical children expressing apprehension about integrated programs, at least one study that included measures at the beginning and end of a school year indicated that these concerns lessened over time (Bailey & Winton, 1987). Other studies reinforce the hypothesis that experience with integrated and inclusive placements lessens initial concerns about this educational model (Diamond & LeFurgy, 1994; Green & Stoneman, 1989).

Among parents of school-aged children with disabilities, dissatisfaction with non-inclusive programs has been the impetus behind court decisions clarifying the least restrictive environment language of the Individuals with Disabilities Education Act (IDEA). In a five year period, four federal appellate courts upheld the right of students with moderate to severe disabilities to be full time members of a general education classroom, with accommodations and supports delivered in this setting (see Appendix A for a description of these cases). The process of obtaining inclusive services, as exemplified by these extended court battles and other evidence (Erwin & Soodak, 1995), suggests that in too many instances, this is an uphill battle for families. Despite their victory in the Third Circuit Court of Appeals, for example, the Oberti family ultimately moved to a new community and sent their children to a private school in order for their son, Rafael, to be included in a school that was eager for him to attend (Schnaiberg, 1996).

What motivates parents to go to such lengths to secure inclusive placements for their children? Two common themes expressed by parents interviewed by Erwin and Soodak (1995) were their desire for their children to belong, and their view of inclusion as a basic right. Positive expectations associated with general class participation (California Research Institute, 1992) are evident in the comments of parents of students with severe disabilities interviewed by Ryndak and colleagues (Ryndak, Downing, Jacqueline, & Morrison, 1995). Similarly, a majority (87.8%) of a sample of parents of students with mild disabilities placed in a collaborative general education classroom expressed a positive response to their child's regular class placement (Lowenbraun, Madge & Affleck, 1990). Not only is there substantial evidence that parents do not see inclusion harming their child's learning and development (e.g., Bailey & Winton, 1989; Green & Stoneman, 1989; Lowenbraun et al., 1990; Peck, Carlson & Helmstetter, 1992), they report that their children benefit from this experience (Giangreco, Edelman, Cloninger & Dennis, 1993c; Miller et al., 1992). A recent study also suggested a spillover effect, with parents of typical children reporting feelings of greater acceptance of others as a result of their child's school experiences (Staub, Schwartz, Gallucci & Peck, 1994).

Parental support for inclusive services, however, is far from universal. Carr, for example, (1995) describes general education placements in which the needs of her son with a learning disability were not addressed. She, like other parents opposed to inclusion, did not see changes occurring in schools to adequately support students with disabilities in regular class placements.

Looking to the future, parents of students with disabilities interviewed by Ryndak et al. (1995) expressed a belief that inclusion was the vehicle whereby positive options would become available to their children. There is some evidence to suggest that these parents may be justified in their optimism. Experience in integrated school programs has been linked to positive post-school outcomes for students with disabilities (e.g., Brown et al., 1987; Hasazi, Gordon & Roe, 1985).

Teacher Perspectives

Substantial effort has been directed toward understanding the attitude of regular classroom teachers toward the placement of students with disabilities in general education settings. A recent synthesis of research (Scruggs & Mastropieri, 1996), based on studies dating back to 1958, indicates that approximately two-thirds of the 10,560 general educators surveyed across the years agreed with the *concept* of mainstreaming/inclusion. Their degree of enthusiasm decreases, however, when the concept is personally referenced [e.g., "Are *you* willing to teach students with disabilities in *your* classroom?" (Whinnery, Fuchs & Fuchs, 1991)]. Support decreases even further when questions address teacher willingness to make curricular modifications for identified students (e.g., Horne, 1983; Houck & Rogers, 1994).

While there is, undoubtedly, validity in these documented trends, the lessons that can be derived from this large body of work are compromised by the lack of contextual information typically gathered in survey research. The answers of teachers from schools in which students with disabilities have been placed into general education classrooms without adequate supports or preparation are likely to be different from teachers working in settings in which special education supports to the general education teacher and students with disabilities in the regular classroom have been provided. This information is simply not consistently available to factor into the interpretation of results.

More recent investigations of teacher perceptions about inclusion deal with actual rather than hypothetical situations. In a sample of 1,152 elementary school teachers who reported to have at least one student with a disability in their class, large discrepancies were noted between the availability and the necessity of training and resources to support these students (Werts, Wolery, Snyder, Caldwell & Salisbury, 1996). In each area queried, needs perceived by teachers greatly exceeded the supports they had reportedly received. Furthermore, unmet needs increased relative to the severity of the disability of the student in their classroom. In contrast, studies involving teachers who reportedly received adequate support and training about inclusion or studies involving teachers who are in co-teaching situations (Minke, Bear, Deemer & Griffin, 1996) describe them as feeling successful and positive about inclusion (e.g., Gemmell-Crosby & Hanzlik, 1994; Wolery, Werts, Caldwell, Snyder & Liskowski, 1995). Similarly, Bennett and colleagues (Bennett,, DeLuca & Bruns, 1997) found a significant relationship between teacher confidence and their ability to access resources and support for inclusion.

The variable of teacher experience and success is considered in other recent attitudinal studies. A sample of ten general educators identified by their peers and principal as being "effective inclusionists" were interviewed in an effort to identify attitudes and attributes associated with their success (Olson, Chalmers & Hoover, 1997). These teachers described themselves as: (a) tolerant, flexible, and reflective; (b) responsible for all students in their classroom; (c) working positively with special educators; and (d) establishing individualized expectations for students in their classroom. In a sample of 84 teachers, a significant relationship was found between the degree to which teachers reported themselves to be successful including students with disabilities, and their attitudes and level of confidence about inclusion.

Finally, a sample of teachers and administrators experienced in inclusion were asked about their perceptions of inclusion (Villa, Thousand, Meyers, & Nevin, 1996). The majority of a sample of 680 general and special educators surveyed responded positively to questions that assessed their belief in the assumptions that underlie inclusion. A majority of respondents believed that general and special educators can work together as partners, and that the achievement of students with disabilities is not diminished in general education classrooms. They also reported increased feelings of competency as a result of their work in teaching teams, feelings also documented by Pugach and Johnson (1995) as outcomes of collaborative teaching.

Examining attitudes about specific implementation issues, Pearman and colleagues (Pearman, Huang & Mellblom, 1997) sought to identify the types of supports that educators feel would enhance their ability to successfully meet the needs of all students. Among a sample of 558 staff within a single school district, the greatest priorities identified by staff were training and funding issues. Specific areas of concern/need involved training to work in a consultative/collaborative model, training about curricular adaptations, reduction in class size, and planning time to support cooperative teaching. Data from a large scale survey conducted in Iowa,

Nebraska and Florida (Hamre-Nietupski, Hendrickson, Nietupski & Shokoohi-Yekta, 1994) explore the issue of teacher responsibility in the social domain. When asked who should be responsible for facilitating friendships between students with and without disabilities, a sample of 312 teachers suggested that adults in the school, including regular educators, can and should be actively involved in facilitating these connections.

Student Perspectives

While much attention has been focused on the response of teachers to the presence of students with disabilities in their classrooms, the perception of typical students about peers with disabilities has also generated a substantial amount of investigation. Based largely on research conducted in integrated preschool settings, early evidence suggested that high levels of interaction between students with and without disabilities did not reliably occur without some type of intervention (Ballard, Corman, Gottlieb & Kaufman, 1978; Devoney, Guralnick & Rubin, 1974), particularly for students with the most severe disabilities (Guralnick, 1980; Sinson & Whetherwick, 1981). Within school settings, researchers found that students with disabilities placed in the regular classroom were not always well accepted by their peers (e.g., Bruininks, 1978; Bryan, 1974, 1978). Fortunately, a wide variety of strategies, including teaching typical peers specific initiation and interaction skills (e.g., Brady, Shores, Gunter, McEvoy, Fox & White, 1984), using cooperative learning structures for small group instruction (e.g., Johnson & Johnson, 1981), and teaching students with disabilities critical social skills (Gresham, 1981), have been found effective in increasing peer interaction in heterogeneous classrooms (see outcome discussion later in this section).

The integration of students with more severe disabilities into regular classrooms stimulated continued efforts to understand the response of typical students to peers with disabilities. Given the hope and expectation that involvement with typical peers would promote social and communication skill development for students with disabilities (Brown, Ford, Nisbet, Sweet, Donnellan & Gruenewald, 1983; Snyder, Apolloni & Cooke, 1977), the extent to which typical students were comfortable in these relationships was critical. In a survey of 2,626 elementary-aged students representing three levels of exposure to such students (i.e., no contact, low contact, high contact), Voeltz (1980) found that upper elementary aged children, girls, and children in schools with the most contact between students expressed the most accepting attitudes toward those with disabilities. Based on the evidence that contact is a critical variable, Voeltz then evaluated the impact of a longitudinal program in which interactions were structured between students with severe disabilities and their typical peers. She found significantly higher acceptance of student differences among students involved in this program as compared with students in schools in which no such students or programs were present (Voeltz, 1982).

Positive attitudes toward students with severe disabilities have also been documented among typical middle and high school students (Peck, Donaldson & Pezzoli, 1990; York, Vandercook, Macdonald, Heise-Neff, & Caughey, 1992). Once again, these findings involve students who had ongoing contact with similar-aged peers with disabilities. Finally, in a large scale survey of middle and high school students, a majority of students indicated a willingness to form friendships with students with severe disabilities. While many students saw themselves as the one who should initiate these relationships, they also expressed the sentiment that these friendships would not be easy to form, and they might not know what to do (Henrickson, Shokoohi-Hekta, Hamre-Nietupski, & Gable, 1996).

Other recent studies have examined student reaction to practices associated with inclusive approaches to education. Crowley (1993) conducted a series of in-depth interviews with six students with behavioral disorders who had been placed in general education classrooms for at least a year prior to this study, supplementing this information with classroom observation. Through these discussions, she was able to capture student perceptions of teacher attitudes and behaviors that they found to be either helpful or not helpful in supporting their placement in general education classrooms. Patterns of teacher-student communication emerged as a predominant theme in student responses. Students identified behaviors such as asking a student's opinion, and communicating clear academic and behavioral expectations as helpful to them. Teaching approaches for both academic and behavioral programming also emerged as themes. Students found teachers who were flexible and provided choices to be most helpful.

Pugach and Wesson (1995) interviewed fifth grade students with and without disabilities who were members of a team-taught classroom. In this highly supportive context, there was no evidence that the general education students even knew who the students with disabilities were. Students with disabilities previously served in a resource room perceived themselves as belonging to their grade level class, doing grade level work (e.g., *"last year I was doin' first-grade stuff, and this year fifth-grade stuff"*, pg. 287) and enjoying school more (e.g., *"When you're in a bigger class, it's funner"*, pg. 287).

While the structure and support provided by teachers in the general education classroom appear key to acceptance, success, and student satisfaction, it is important to remember the fears associated with new types of placements for all students involved. Jenkins and Heinen (1989) have documented the preference of students with mild disabilities to receive instruction in the settings with which they have the most experience, even if they do not afford opportunities for involvement with their typical peers. Similarly, Tymitz-Wolf (1984) describes the worries and fears expressed by students with mild disabilities prior to general class placement. These concerns encompass both social and academic issues.

Responses to Accommodating Differences in the Classroom

Beyond the issue of attitudes, there is a large body of research that examines general educator willingness and capability to provide accommodations necessary to meet the needs of diverse learners. A substantial number of these investigations have focused on *whether* and *how* general educators can become better equipped to meet individual student needs. While providing fuel for those who believe that general educators are unlikely to "learn a monumental number of additional skills in order to deal with both special and regular education students (Smelter et al., pg. 38), this literature also provides valuable lessons for those seeking to avoid mistakes of the past.

There is a considerable amount of evidence that general educators leave their teacher education program unprepared to respond to the range of student abilities represented in most classrooms today (Goodland & Field, 1993; Rosjewski & Pollard, 1990; Willliams, 1990). Furthermore, teachers do not readily acquire these skills simply as a function of experience. Findings indicate that teachers tend to:

◆ plan instructional lessons for the whole class without considering the needs of individual students (Vaughn & Schumm, 1994);

◆ rely heavily on large group instruction, not differentiating instruction based on the individual needs of students (Baker & Zigmond, 1990; McIntosh, Vaughn, Schumm, Haager & Lee, 1994); and

◆ rate instructional adaptations as more desirable than they are feasible (Schumm & Vaughn, 1991).

A pessimistic interpretation of this research is that individualization and instructional adaptation are simply incompatible with the prevailing structure of the general education classroom (e.g., Baker & Zigmond, 1990; Fuchs, Fuchs, Hamlett, Phillips & Karns, 1995). Viewed in light of reports that general education teachers prefer pull-out special education programs (e.g., Coates, 1989; Semmel, Abernathy, Butera & Lesar, 1991), it is easy to conclude that the push for more inclusive service models is unrealistic. However, an examination of the context of these studies leads to other interpretations. These investigations were conducted in settings with little to low levels of interaction between general education and special education teachers. In the series of studies conducted by Schumm and Vaughn, students with learning disabilities were served in a pull-out model. Teachers were not involved in systematic and regular consultation or collaboration (Schumm, Vaughn, Haager, McDowell,

Rothlein & Saumell, 1995). In one study (Vaughn & Schumm, 1994), the authors indicated that the general education teacher in their sample did not even know who the special education students were until the second or third month of school! There are, then, other intervening factors that could contribute to these teacher behaviors.

In contrast, in settings where supports are available to general educators, documented results are far more positive. A study conducted by Giangreco and colleagues (Giangreco, Dennis, Cloninger, Edelman & Schattman, 1993b) highlights the importance of experience and support in altering perceptions about inclusive placements. Using qualitative methodology, 19 general educators who had at least one student with severe disabilities as a full-time member of their class within the past three years were interviewed regarding their experiences. Teachers reported a very cautious or negative reaction to the placement at the beginning of the school year. All but two of the teachers evidenced a "transformation" throughout the year, leading to increased ownership and involvement with their new student, as well as perceived benefits to themselves and professionals.

Evolution of Models to Support General Education Teachers

In the literature considered thus far, teacher support emerges as a critical factor associated with the success of general class placement for students with disabilities. The way in which this support is provided, then, should be carefully considered. There has been an evolution in thinking about approaches to providing support, influenced by the increasing number of students for whom placement in the general education classroom is occurring, and the intensity of support needed by some students.

Consulting Teacher Models

Friend (1988) points to the growing dissatisfaction with segregated special education services and a rapidly increasing number of students in need of specialized support as two of the forces contributing to the use of special educators as consultants to their general education colleagues. As is currently evident in the professional discussion about inclusion, varied approaches to consultation exist. Despite this variation, two goals are common to all models: (a) problem-solving that addresses immediate concerns; and (b) increasing the capacity of the consultee in order to prevent or respond more effectively to similar situations in the future (West & Idol, 1987).

Clarifying what the model is and is not, Huefner (1988) underscored the *indirect* nature of this service, and the potential problems that could occur if these parameters are violated.

If the special education teacher merely "takes over" for the regular teacher and instructs a certain number of children for a portion of the regular teacher's day, the chances to share are diluted and the particular skills of the consulting teacher underutilized. ...The goal is not to relieve the regular education teacher from the responsibility for teaching difficult students (Huefner, 1988, pg. 404).

If the consulting model includes direct, substantive service to students in the regular classroom on a continuing basis, there will be pressure to turn the model into a classroom tutoring or aide model, underutilizing the consulting teacher's potential contribution to regular education programs in general (pg. 407).

The tremendous variation in implementation models and other key variables makes it difficult to synthesize the literature about consultation (Gresham & Kendall, 1987). Nevertheless, available research regarding special education consultation (e.g., Hanley & Everitt, 1977; Idol-Maestas, 1983; Idol-Maestas & Jackson, 1983; Knight, Meyers, Paolucci-Whitcomb, Hasazi, & Nevin, 1981; Miller & Sabatino, 1978; Nelson & Stevens, 1981; Wixson, 1980) suggests positive changes at the teacher, student, and system levels as a result of consultative services (West & Idol, 1987), although the rigor of this evidence has been challenged (Huefner, 1988).

A subset of the consultation research literature is specifically focused on how to provide effective support to general educators. The following themes emerge from this group of studies:

◆ *more is better:* general educators valued supports from special educators that went beyond suggestions to accommodate students' needs (Fuchs, Fuchs, Behr, Fernstrom & Stecker, 1990; Speece & Mandell, 1980);

◆ *experience is a good teacher:* interaction about students leads to increased feelings of teacher competence (Miller & Sabatino, 1978);

◆ *trust:* a constructive climate of mutual trust is critical to effective consultation (Friend, 1984);

◆ *resources and training:* barriers to effective consultation include inadequate time, and lack of administrative support (Idol-Maestas & Ritter, 1985; Kratochwill & Van Someren, 1985; Nevin, Paolucci-Whitcomb, Duncan & Thibodeau, 1982);

◆ *skills:* consultation requires effective communication and problem-solving skills (Conoley & Conoley, 1982; DeBoer, 1986; Rosenfield, 1987); and

◆ *role definition:* role ambiguity is associated with undue teacher stress (Crane & Iwanicki, 1986).

While this research underscores the need for consistent and ongoing supportive interactions between general and special educators in a consultative relationship, available evidence suggests that in practice, the lack of time, administrative support, and preparation threaten the integrity of this form of support. In many schools, resource room teachers are given the responsibility for consultation with general educators, yet their pull-out caseloads are not reduced to enable them to adequately do so (Johnson, Pugach & Hammittee, 1988; Kratochwill & Van Someren, 1985). As a result, contacts between consultants and general educators are often brief, forcing the consultants to rely heavily on their own perceptions of the problem and intervention priorities (Gans, 1985).

Collaborative Consultation

Most consultative models are based on the presumption that the consultant is an expert who brings specialized information to a problematic situation. In a school setting, this creates a hierarchical relationship between the special and general educator, in which the expectation is that the general educator is ready, willing, and able to implement recommendations made by the specialist. Evidence already reviewed indicates that this is not always the case. Johnson and colleagues (Johnson et al., 1988) suggest this dissonance can be explained by: (a) the special educator's lack of credibility *relative to the general education classroom;* (b) mismatches between the thinking of the special education consultant and classroom teacher; (c) the hierarchical nature of the consultative relationship; and (d) the differing knowledge bases of general and special educators.

In response to the dissatisfaction with an expert model, the term *collaborative consultation* has emerged to describe support delivered within the context of an equitable relationship. Summarizing evaluation reports of collaborative consultation models, Idol and colleagues (Idol, Nevin & Paolucci-Whitcomb,1994) present evidence of its effectiveness at the preschool (e.g., Peck, Killen & Baumgart, 1989), elementary (e.g., Adamson, Cox & Schuller, 1989; Schulte, Osborne & McKinney, 1990), and secondary school levels (e.g., Florida Department of Education, 1989, 1990). All of these efforts were focused on meeting the needs of students with mild to moderate disabilities in general education classrooms. The work of Giangreco et al. (1993) reports similarly positive outcomes in supporting students with more severe disabilities.

Co-Teaching

While collaborative approaches to teacher support build upon multiple perspectives and sources of expertise in planning instruction, the implementation of jointly planned approaches remains the responsibility of the general educator. As classrooms become even more diverse and the demands placed upon the general educator increase, collaborative support may, in some cases, not be enough. In situations where there are large numbers of students with special needs and/or students with intense needs, the involvement of specialists in both the planning and implementation of services is required. Bauwens, Hourcade and Friend (1989) describe this approach as cooperative teaching or co-teaching.

Co-teaching was a popular model during the era of open schools. Initial indicators of its value as a special education support model are promising. Pugach and Wesson (1995) gathered both teacher and student perspectives to evaluate two fifth grade team taught classes. Students and teachers were similarly positive in their reviews. Students reported that teachers created a motivating learning environment, while teachers described themselves as confident about meeting the needs of all students in their classroom. Walter-Thomas (1997) evaluated the impact of co-teaching models in 23 schools across eight school districts. She reported positive outcomes relative to the academic and social skills of low-achieving students, improved attitudes and self-concepts reported by students with disabilities, and the development of positive peer relationships. Students perceived that these gains were a result of more teacher time and attention. Both special and general educators reported professional growth, personal support, and enhanced teaching motivation, and general educators reported a greater "sense of community" in their classrooms. Finally, in a direct comparison of a pull-out support model with one in which special educators teach within the general education classroom, Meyers, Glezheiser and Yelich (1991) found classroom teachers to prefer the in-class support model. They reported more frequent collaborative meetings, a greater focus on instructional issues, and acquisition of more instructional techniques to support students with diverse learning needs.

While the potential advantages to this approach are apparent, teachers surveyed about its implementation cite concerns about time, the ability to develop cooperative working relationships, and the perception that this approach would increase their workload as anticipated obstacles (Bauwens et al., 1989). Teachers in the Walter-Thomas (1997) study identified the lack of staff development activities as a drawback to their experience.

Research About the Implementation Process

The experience of educators actively engaged in the adoption of inclusive approaches to education is a rich source of lessons to guide others in the process. Information derived from published accounts describing efforts at multiple sites, individual buildings and classrooms, and districts is summarized in this section.

Multi-Site Studies

In a study designed to extract lessons from practitioners in schools adopting an inclusive approach to educating students with moderate to severe disabilities, Janney and colleagues (Janney, Snell, Beers & Raynes, 1995) sampled personnel from 10 schools in five districts in Virginia. These schools had been part of a statewide project that provided technical assistance and consultation. Thus, this study draws upon the experience of schools that wanted to change their practices, and received assistance in helping them do so. Based on the results of semi-structured interviews with 53 teachers and administrators, the authors identified themes that are reported in the form of "advice" to school personnel. Their recommendations are summarized in Table 11.

Table 11
Advice Themes For School Personnel Adopting an Inclusive Model[7]

Advice for District Administrators	Advice for Principals
◆ Give a "green light" to do what's best for all students. ◆ Direct without dictating.	◆ Set a positive tone. ◆ Start with teacher volunteers. ◆ Involve everyone in preparation and planning. ◆ Provide information, orientation, and training. ◆ Provide resources and handle the logistics. ◆ Start small and build. ◆ Give teachers the freedom to do it.
Advice for General Educators	**Advice for Special Educators**
◆ Have an open mind. ◆ Problem-solve as a team. ◆ Help the student to belong.	◆ Be personable and flexible in working with others to support students. ◆ Provide task-related supports to receiving teachers (e.g., information, advise).

[7]From: Janney et al., 1995, pgs. 431-435.

Building-Level Implementation Efforts

Many other studies chronicle the change process within a single building. As illustrated in Table 12, they vary in scope, ranging from a longitudinal study focused on a single student (e.g., Kozleski & Jackson, 1993), to efforts focused on a specific population of students with disabilities (e.g., Baker, 1995a). Other studies examined school-wide initiatives, encompassing all identified students with disabilities (e.g., Salisbury, Palombaro & Hollowood, 1993; Zigmond, 1995a).

As discussed in earlier sections of this document, the tremendous variation in what is called "inclusion" is aptly illustrated by this group of studies. This is most evident in the studies focused on students with learning disabilities, published in a topical issue of the Journal of Special Education entitled "Case Studies of Full Inclusion for Students with Learning Disabilities". The authors acknowledge that the only common element to define inclusion across the five sites studies was the placement site (i.e., the general education classroom). Focus on this single dimension as a selection critieria fails to acknowledge the other values and practices that characterize inclusive education models (see discussion of definitions in Part I). In this context, if the regular classroom was the primary site in which education was provided, any approach to delivering instruction to students with disabilities was characterized as *inclusion*. Under these circumstances, the conclusion of the authors and several reviewers that inclusive programs compromise the "special" in special education is not too surprising (Gerber, 1995; Martin, 1995; Zigmond & Baker, 1995).

Table 12
Case Studies Focused on Building-Level Change

Author(s)	Scope of Intervention
Baker, 1995a	Inclusion of students with learning disabilities at the elementary level in Virginia.
Baker, 1995b	Inclusion of students with learning disabilities at the elementary and intermediate level in Minnesota.
Baker, 1995c	Inclusion of students with learning disabilities at the elementary level in Washington.
Fox & Ysseldyke, 1997	Inclusion of students with mild/moderate mental retardation in a middle school.
Kozleski & Jackson, 1993	Inclusion of a student with severe disabilities in an elementary school (documented grades 3 through 5).
Salisbury et al., 1993	Inclusion of students with disabilities in an elementary school in Johnson City, New York.
Tralli, Colombo, Deshler & Schumaker, 1996	Inclusion of students with mild disabilities at the secondary level in Clayton, Missouri.
Zigmond, 1995a	Inclusion of students with learning disabilities at the elementary level in Pennsylvania.
Zigmond, 1995b	Inclusion of students with learning disabilities at the elementary level in Kansas.

While it would be easy to simply dismiss some of these case studies by concluding *"this is not really inclusion"*, they do represent initial attempts to change the way in which services are provided to students with mild disabilities. A critical analysis of the role changes, supports, and strategies described can be instructive in highlighting issues to consider in planning for change, and affirming available information about essential supports for meaningful change. In Table 13, observations drawn from the case studies are presented alongside prevailing best practice recommendations drawn from the inclusive schooling practices literature.

Table 13
Case Study Observations as Compared to Inclusion "Best Practices"

Case Study Observations	Inclusion "Best Practices"
1. Teacher Roles and Interaction	
◆ Role changes predominantly focused on special educator; special educators identified as members of a grade level team in some in coteaching situations (e.g., Baker, 1995b). ◆ Coteaching took many different forms across sites.	◆ In inclusive schools, general and special educators share responsibility for meeting the needs of all students in a class (Thousand & Villa, 1990). ◆ There are many ways in which teachers can divide responsibilities in a co-teaching arrangement. "One teach/one support" does not maximize the talents of both participants (Friend & Cooke, 1996).
◆ In one example (Kozleski & Jackson, 1993) active general educator involvement in curricular accommodations is described, and is associated with high levels of classroom participation; in others, responsibility appears to fall entirely on the special educator.	◆ Teachers collaborate at the instructional planning phase, so that planning for diversity is "front loaded" (Heron & Jorgenson, 1995; Jorgensen, 1996; Udvari-Solner, 1995).
◆ Studies focused on students with learning disabilities utilized categorical models of delivering special education supports (e.g., Baker, 1995a,b; Zigmond, 1995a,b).	◆ Non-categorical approaches to special education support maximize the time that a special educator can spend in a general education classroom (York-Barr, Kronberg, & Doyle, 1996).
◆ Availability of planning time varied across sites from planning "on the fly" (Baker, 1995b) to regularly scheduled time for the purpose (e.g., Baker, 1995a; Salisbury et al., 1993).	◆ Time must be available to discuss ongoing instructional plans, providing an opportunity to adapt instruction/materials as needed (Thousand & Villa, 1995).
◆ Special education support within the classroom ranged from 30 min/day to 2 hours/day in the studies involving students with learning disabilities.	◆ Special education support personnel must be in the classroom for a long enough period of time for them to be useful to the teacher. Regular education teachers can't rely upon them as teaching partners if their presence is sporadic or too brief (Friend & Cook, 1996).

Case Study Observations	Inclusion "Best Practices"
2. Scope of Change	
◆ While moving toward inclusion, some schools maintained cluster programs to justify more special education staff positions (Baker, 1995a,c; Zigmond, 1995b).	◆ The principle of natural proportions underlies the emphasis on home school placement for students with disabilities (Brown et al., 1989). If students with disabilities attend the school they naturally would attend if not identified as disabled, each school would have manageable numbers of students with disabilities to support.
◆ Clusters of students were placed in general education classrooms to increase the time special educators could spend there and/or because these teachers "volunteered" to teach such a class (Baker, 1995a,b; Zigmond, 1995b).	◆ A school-wide philosophy that articulates the rights and ability of all children to learn (Schlechty, 1990) establishes a foundation in which all teachers work together to teach all students (Thousand & Villa, 1990).
◆ Most studies focused on only certain "categories" of students (e.g., Tralli et al., 1996); several indicated building-wide changes (Salisbury et al., 1993; Zigmond, 1995a).	◆ Belonging is a central tenet of inclusion (Kunc, 1992), contributing to the belief system that drives other decisions and actions of a school (Falvey, Givner & Kimm, 1995). With such a foundation, an inclusive approach to education begins with general education placement as the first option for all students.
◆ With one exception (Salisbury et al., 1993), the inclusion effort was not described as being linked with larger building or district-level reform initiatives.	◆ The changes required of schools to meet the needs of students with disabilities are congruent with the changes necessary for classrooms to be responsive to the needs of all learners (Jorgensen & Fried, 1994; Lipsky & Gartner, 1997). The needs of students with disabilities should be considered within the context of general education reform rather than as a separate system (Consortium for Inclusive Schooling Practices, 1996).

Case Study Observations	Inclusion "Best Practices"
3. Curriculum and Instructional Practices	
◆ Basic skills approach to general education instruction characterized many of the sites (e.g., Baker, 1995a; Zigmond, 1995b); instructional practices known to accommodate diverse learners were a part of some models (e.g., Baker, 1995b, Salisbury et al., 1993b).	◆ Best practice in general education involves active, meaningful, and integrated approaches to instruction (Zemelman, Daniels & Hyde, 1993).
◆ Whole group instruction predominanted many of the site descriptions.	◆ All students learn differently, and classroom instruction should be planned and delivered in a way that actively acknowledges this fact (Cohen, 1994; Jorgensen, 1996; Stainback, Stainback, Stefanich & Alper, 1996). Students with disabilities in inclusive classrooms are more engaged in 1:1, small group, and independent work arrangements than during whole class instruction (Logan, Bakeman & Keefe, 1997).
4. Preparation and Ongoing Support for Change	
◆ Site support ranged from training and fiscal support from a university/SEA (Zigmond, 1995a) to local model development without outside involvement (Baker, 1995a).	◆ A school district can gain valuable human, political, and fiscal resources by developing partnerships with local universities, other school districts, and/or the state department of education to support the change effort (Thousand & Villa, 1995).
◆ Initial inservice training described in one study (Fox & Ysseldyke, 1997); identified need for ongoing training and support.	◆ Ongoing training and technical assistance is critical to support faculty in adopting new roles and utilizing new skills (Cheney & Harvey, 1994; Schaffner & Buswell, 1996).
◆ Only one study (Salisbury et al., 1993) with a longitudinal focus describes ongoing dialogue and reflection about school practices, leading to fine tuning and changes. The approach is evolutionary and dynamic.	◆ Change is a dynamic process. Working to establish a "culture of inquiry" in a school is a valuable part of the change process (Brubacher, Case & Reagan, 1994).

In reviewing these case study examples, the work of Salisbury and her colleagues in the Johnson City School District emerges as the best single exemplar of building-wide change embedded within a general education reform context. A vision for change was articulated and shared among teachers and administrators. This led to change occurring within a context of collaborative decision-making.   Further, a climate of ongoing dialogue and reflection distinguish this effort from the other documented studies. Strong outcome measures are not a part of any of these reports, although social and academic outcomes of the Johnson City site are described elsewhere (e.g., Evans, Salisbury, Palombaro, Berryman & Hollowood, 1992; Hollowood, Salisbury, Rainforth & Palombaro, 1994;1995; Vickery, 1987), and are highlighted in the next section of this document.

The varying perspectives and scope of these efforts reflect distinct differences in purpose. The group of studies focused exclusively on students with learning disabilities was clearly motivated by an interest in understanding whether this group of students is well served in an inclusion model (Zigmond, 1995). Other efforts were motivated by an interest to better understand variables that impact implementation and maintenance of an approach, firmly grounded in the belief that inclusion is an appropriate goal for special education (e.g., Kozleski & Jackson, 1993; Salisbury et al., 1993) and a necessary characteristic of schools for all students. Underneath these varying philosophies are very different expectations about the degree to which education must change if inclusion is the goal. In reacting to the case studies focused on students with learning disabilities, Pugach (1995) writes:

> *Without question, more does have to change if inclusion is the goal, and the changes required are greater, and more fundamental, than ever before. So while debates over the appropriateness of inclusion as special education policy continue to be rancorous, these are not really debates about the merits of inclusion as a basic philosophy or ethical stance. Rather, they are debates over the degree of optimism various stakeholders have regarding the capacity for the educational system - which includes special and general education alike - to recreate itself with inclusion as a basic premise and achievement as a tangible goal* (pgs. 212-213).

District-Level Implementation Efforts

Case studies focusing on entire districts suggest a substantial commitment to reform and restructuring, and a realization that the changes required to create inclusive schools go far beyond the placement of a small group of students. Table 14 identifies published descriptions exemplifying these larger-scale efforts, as well as strategies and outcomes that have been documented. A comparison of the processes and strategies used in these five examples yields several common elements: (a) a strong values base that grounds the change effort; (b) a strong and ongoing commitment to support personnel to learn the necessary skills to work in new ways; (c) efforts to include previously segregated students occurred in an environment of general education reform; (d) role changes occurred for all teaching staff, not just special educators; and (e) change was planful, occurring across a number of years.

Table 14
District-Level Inclusion Implementation Studies/Descriptions

Focus	Process/Strategies	Lessons Learned
◆ Restructuring of **Winooski (VT)** school district to accommodate diversity of all students (Cross & Villa, 1992).	◆ Instructional services are delivered to all students in general education settings through team teaching, consultation, and collaborative arrangements among teachers; use of classroom aides and peer tutors; accommodations for individual learners; and curricular modifications. ◆ Adoption of mission statement was supported by comprehensive inservice training agenda designed to support teachers to realize vision of mission statement. ◆ Students were returned from out of district placements over a four year period of time. ◆ Staff roles changed; single teacher job description; integration and support facilitator role was established. ◆ Administrative structure was redefined to better coordinate services.	◆ Cooperation between teaching staff and district administration is essential. ◆ Implementation process is evolutionary, grounded in a mission statement supportive of inclusive schooling.
◆ Understand/describe movement of students with moderate/severe disabilities from self-contained classes to general education classes in their home in **St. Cloud, Minnesota** (York-Barr , Schultz, Doyle, Kronberg & Crossett, 1996).	◆ Strategic planning for inclusion was a response to multiple, precipitation influences. ◆ Focus on people-aspect of change, supporting the definition of new roles and responsibilities, and leadership in the change process. ◆ Focus on sharing success, maintenance of change efforts, and ongoing administrative support.	◆ Successful educational reform focuses on people not just structure. ◆ There is more to effective teaching than classroom management and instructional competence. ◆ Teachers can be agents of social change.

Focus	Process/Strategies	Lessons Learned
◆ District-wide effort in **Saline Area Schools (MI)** to include students with severe disabilities in home schools (Kaskinen-Chapman, 1992).	◆ History of serving students with mild disabilities in home schools. ◆ Redefined job functions of special educators who had taught in segregated classrooms. ◆ Ongoing opportunities for staff to air their concerns. ◆ Based model on known "best practices", including collaborative support teams, student peer support networks, use of effective instructional practices in general education classes, and networks of supports for teachers.	◆ Self-examination of beliefs in the principles of equity, integrity, human dignity, service, excellence, and potential provided impetus and energy to undertake this level of change. ◆ Recognition that ongoing restructuring of schools is a necessity.
◆ District-wide policy to include students with emotional/ behavioral disorders was adopted in a **Northern New England City;** study documents outcomes of this policy over a five year period of time (Cheney & Harvey, 1994).	◆ District had previously been involved in effort to integrate students with severe disabilities in general education settings. ◆ Reallocation of funds to hire more support personnel as reliance on out-of-district placement decreased. ◆ District-wide needs assessment informed staff development activities. ◆ "Wraparound" meetings conducted to coordinate services across agencies.	◆ Importance of long term staff development, with focus on dealing with complex student behavior. ◆ Efforts were complemented by other regular education reforms, including heterogeneous grouping, literature-based reading, and outcome-based measurement. ◆ Ongoing interagency collaboration to provide wraparound services.

Focus	Process/Strategies	Lessons Learned
◆ District-wide effort in **Franklin Northwest Supervisory Union (VT)** to return students with severe disabilities to their home schools (Schattman, 1992)	◆ Shift toward inclusive practices stimulated by changes initiated by adoption of outcomes-based model of instruction, funding changes that supported inclusion, adoption of collaborative teaming practices and initial successes. ◆ Established link with university technical assistance project ◆ Transition planning process to identify necessary supports to return students to their home district/school	◆ Collaborative teams capitalize upon the best thinking of all of its members. ◆ Teaming is enough of a priority that time is found to support this activity. ◆ You're never really there - there is need for constant growth and improvement. ◆ System-wide inclusion is very different from student-specific integration, suggesting systemic supports to facilitate transitions, and an ongoing *expectation* for inclusion to occur.

A final program description to be reviewed is singular in its scope, emphasizing the leadership role of the state department of education in Colorado, and the many partnerships that have been established to provide a policy and practice environment which fosters sound inclusive services (McNulty, Rogers-Connolly, Wilson & Brewer, 1996). Grounded in a value system that favors general class placement within the neighborhood school, multiple initiatives were designed to reduce the barriers to serving students with disabilities in these settings.

Strategies were developed to address the needs of students who were already in regular schools but in segregated placements, as well as those students who were currently served in separate settings. These included assistance-based initiatives to help school personnel move from a disability/placement mindset to one focused on identifying student needs and necessary supports. State funding practices were changed to channel all special education dollars directly to districts, who then had the option to use those dollars to contract out for services/placements for students served in segregated settings, or to use those dollars to provide supports locally. Similarly, funding changes in the area of transportation brought together "special ed" and "regular ed" transportation dollars, enabling these funds to be used to make regular busses accessible rather than run two separate transportation systems. In concert with these policy initiatives, other partnerships resulted in securing federal dollars to provide technical assistance at the building and district level to adopt more inclusive practices. These activities are supporting existing school-improvement initiatives, so that inclusion becomes a part of these broad-based restructuring agendas. The effort described in this program description exemplifies the coordination and alignment of efforts along multiple fronts to achieve a vision of educational practice that has a strong values base. At a time when local control is increasingly valued, this example illustrates how state leadership and local control can co-exist.

Outcomes of Inclusive Schooling Practices

In this final section, research is summarized that demonstrates the positive impact of inclusive schooling practices on its participants - students, teachers, and families, as well as the programmatic structures involved. The discussion will highlight themes describing what has been empirically documented to date, and what has been learned about how to maximize positive outcomes. Readers interested in more methodological detail about specific studies cited in each outcome area can refer to the series of descriptive tables contained in Appendix B. These tables do not include articles which are, themselves, research reviews, meta-analyses, or snytheses.

Skill Acquisition for Students with Disabilities

Lloyd Dunn's article questioning the efficacy of resource room placement for students with mild mental retardation (1968) is among the most widely cited in the field of special education, continuing to stimulate discussion, research, and changes in policy and practice in the years since its publication (MacMillan, Semmel & Gerber, 1995). Dunn and many others have stressed the availability of students who can serve as role models and initiators of communication and social interaction as an important reason to place students with disabilities in general education classrooms. It is not surprising, therefore, that much of the initial research examining outcomes for students with disabilities placed in general education classrooms focused on these skill areas. The themes describe below reflect evidence available to date.

■ *Students with disabilities demonstrate high levels of social interaction in settings with their typical peers, but placement alone does not guarantee positive social outcomes.*

A substantial number of studies have demonstrated that students with disabilities do interact more frequently in integrated and inclusive settings (e.g., Brinker, 1985; Brinker & Thorpe, 1986; Fryxell & Kennedy, 1995) than in self-contained environments. These results have been demonstrated for children in preschool (Guralnick & Groom, 1988; Hanline, 1993; Jenkins, Odom & Speltz, 1989), elementary (Cole & Meyers, 1991; Fryxell & Kennedy, 1995), and secondary settings (Kennedy, Shukla & Fryxell, 1997; McDonnell, Hardman, Hightower, & Kiefer-O'Donnell, 1991). Despite the opportunities created by the presence of students without disabilities in general education settings, there have been multiple demonstrations that suggest without adult intervention, students without disabilities tend to interact more frequently with their typical peers in social situations (e.g., Faught, Belleweg, Crow & van den Pol, 1983; Odom & Strain, 1986; Sale & Carey,

1995). Fortunately, many strategies have been successfully used to encourage and maintain ongoing interaction between students with and without disabilities, including the use of communication aids and play organizers (Jolly, Text & Spooner, 1993), teacher-mediated interaction (Strain & Odom, 1986), and peer-mediated assists (e.g., Brady, Shores, Gunter, McEvoy, Fox & White, 1984; Sasso & Rude, 1987).

At least two studies suggest that the number of students with disabilities in the classroom has an impact on the level of social interaction that occurs between students with and without disabilities. In a study at the preschool level, Guralnick and Groom (1988) found that the proportion of typical children to students with disabilities had an impact on child interactions. They emphasized the importance of having adequate numbers of typical peers in play groups, providing some empirical support for the principle of "natural proportions" (Brown et al., 1989). Similarly, McDonnell et al. (1991) found that the number of students with severe disabilities in a school was negatively associated with in-school and after school integration. Students placed in their home school had significantly higher levels of interaction with typical peers than those enrolled in cluster programs.

■   *Social competence and communication skills improve when students with disabilities are educated in inclusive settings.*

Closely associated with opportunities for social interaction is growth in social competence and communication skills. Studies documenting parental reports of child development have consistently identified improvement in the area of social skills and communication as outcomes associated with participation in an educational program with typical peers (e.g., Bennett, DeLuca & Bruns, 1997; Guralnick, Connor & Hammond, 1995; Turnbull et al., 1982). These gains have also been documented in studies that directly measure performance in these areas. In a two-year comparison study of students with disabilities in both integrated and segregated settings, Cole and Meyer (1991) found that students in integrated educational placements demonstrated substantial progress on a measure of social competence, encompassing such specific communication and social skills as initiation, self-regulation, choice, and terminating contact. In contrast, comparison students in segregated settings showed regression in these areas across the two year period. Performance gains in these areas have been noted in other placement comparison studies (e.g., Jenkins, Odom & Speltz, 1989), as well as in non-comparison studies conducted in inclusive classroom settings (e.g., Hunt, Alwell, Farron-Davis & Goetz, 1996; Hunt, Staub, Alwell & Goetz, 1994; Jolly, Test & Spooner, 1993; Kozleski & Jackson, 1993).

■   *Students with disabilities have demonstrated gains in other areas of development when they are educated in inclusive settings.*

A series of comparison studies focused on the written educational plan for students with disabilities revealed that students served in general education settings had higher quality IEPs than those who were placed in self-contained classrooms (Hunt & Farron-Davis, 1992; Hunt, Goetz & Anderson, 1986; Hunt, Farron-Davis, Beckstead, Curtis & Goetz, 1994). The last study in this series (Hunt et al., 1994) went the next logical step, observing student performance across settings to compare performance, documenting the level of engagement, involvement in integrated activities, affective demeanor, and social interaction of students in segregated and integrated settings. The inclusive settings were associated with more favorable outcomes on these measures, suggesting greater opportunity for skill development in a variety of curricular areas by virtue of the more varied and stimulating experiences available to students.

Do these opportunities lead to skill acquisition? A recent study investigated the level of academic engagement of students with severe disabilities included in the general education classroom for content-area classes by comparing the behavior of students with disabilities to a sample of peers without disabilities in the same settings (McDonnell, Thorson, McQuivey & Kiefer-O'Donnell, 1997). Despite higher levels of competing behaviors among students with disabilities, there were no significant differences in academic engagement between the two groups of students. While no measures of skill acquisition were reported, these findings are consistent with parent reports that their children are learning material from the general education curriculum as a result of their inclusive placement (Ryndak et al., 1995).

Skill acquisition data in academic areas are more frequently reported in studies that involve the general classroom placement of students with mild disabilities. McDougall and Brady (1998) demonstrated increases in math fluency and engaged time for students with and without disabilities after the introduction of a multi-component self-management intervention. On a larger scale, there are program models for which substantial performance gains for students with disabilities have been found (e.g., Wang & Birch, 1984) as well as those for which positive gains were evidenced in some, but not all, curricular areas (e.g., Affleck, Madge, Adams & Lowenbraun, 1988), or for some, but not all, students with mild disabilities (e.g., Zigmond & Baker, 1990). Manset and Semmel (1997) conclude that gains for students <u>without</u> disabilities are the most consistent outcome of this body of research, suggesting the potential benefits of blending the instructional expertise of general and special educators for the benefit of all students, while underscoring the need to pay greater attention to specific organizational and instructional practices in heterogeneous classrooms.

■   *Interactive, small group contexts facilitate skill acquisition and social acceptance for students with disabilities in general education classrooms.*

The traditional general education classroom, with an emphasis on whole group instruction, is increasingly being viewed as a barrier to the learning of not only students with disabilities, but others in the general education classroom that have diverse learning styles. There is a substantial body of evidence that points to instructional groupings that are advantageous for both students with and without disabilities. Wang and Birch (1984) describe the difference in student behavior in a traditionally structured classroom and a classroom designed to accommodate diverse learners (Adaptive Learning Environments Model). In the ALEM classroom, students were more actively engaged in exploratory and individual activities, spending less time in whole group and teacher prescribed activities. The small group structuring associated with cooperative learning has been repeatedly demonstrated as academically (e.g., Lew, Mesch, Johnson & Johnson, 1986; Madden & Slavin, 1983b) and socially beneficial for heterogeneous groups of students (Johnson, Johnson & Anderson, 1983; Johnson & Johnson, 1981; Johnson, Johnson, Tiffany & Zaidman, 1983). Similarly, small group structures associated with peer tutoring are associated with benefits for students with and without disabilities in a variety of academic areas (e.g., Cohen, Kulik & Kulik, 1982; Maheady, Sacca & Harper, 1987; Mathur & Rutherford, 1991; Osguthorpe & Scruggs, 1986).

Several studies have examined the impact of small instructional groups on the skill acquisition of students with more severe disabilities in inclusive settings (Dugan, Kamps, Leonard, Watkins, Rheinberger & Stackhouse, 1995; Hunt et al., 1994; Logan, Bakeman & Keefe, 1997). Hunt and colleagues (Hunt et al., 1994) structured cooperative learning groups involving students with severe disabilities and their typical peers. Students with disabilities learned and generalized the skills targeted for them in this instructional context. Their typical peers performed as well as peers assigned to groups that did not have a student with a severe disability as a group member. In a comparison of whole group, 1:1, individual work, and small group work, similarly positive findings are documented by Dugan et al. (1995). Logan, Bakeman and Keefe (1997) found whole group instruction to be the least favorable context for promoting task engagement of students with severe disabilities. Together, these studies provide some preliminary evidence that the type of instruction currently considered to represent good practice in general education (see Part II) is also, when appropriately structured, conducive to the learning of students with disabilities (Cosden & Haring, 1992).

Social Outcomes for Students with Disabilities

Another powerful rationale for inclusion is that students with disabilities will have the opportunity to develop relationships with peers that evolve into true friendships, carrying over into after school hours. The observations that can be made on the basis of research conducted to date are encompassed within the discussion of three themes below.

■   *Friendships do develop between students with disabilities and their typical peers in inclusive settings.*

There is a body of research that has examined friendship outcomes for students with disabilities based upon their educational placements. A direct comparison of the social interactions, social support behaviors, and friendship networks of students placed in general education classrooms with similar students served in self-contained classrooms clearly favored those in inclusive settings (Fryxell & Kennedy, 1995; Kennedy, Shukla & Fryxell, 1997). Students in inclusive placements had more frequent interaction with their peers, and larger, more durable networks of peers without disabilities. Furthermore, a positive relationship has been established between the proximity of a student's educational placement to his home and in-school and after school involvement with peers (McDonnell et al., 1991). Students who were in integrated settings, but placed in a cluster program, had significantly lower levels of peer involvement than students with disabilities attending their "home" school. These findings again speak to the "best practice" guidelines delineated by Brown and colleagues relative to natural proportion and home school placements (Brown et al., 1989).

Other research about friendship in inclusive settings has been descriptive, providing insight into the type of relationships that develop between students with disabilities and their typical peers. Qualitative investigations describe friendships between students with and without disabilities that show the same variation in relationships and status that one sees in friendships between students without disabilities (Evans et al., 1992; Staub, Schwartz, Gallucci & Peck, 1994). This research suggests that differences seen in relationships are influenced by factors not uniquely associated with disability status.

Using multiple methodologies and data sources gathered over a three year time frame, Meyer and her colleagues (Meyer, Monondo, Fisher, Larson, Dunmore, Black & D'Aquanni, 1998) also found substantial variations in the social relationships occurring between students with severe disabilities and their peers. They identified six distinct "frames" that characterize the relationships they saw. While some of the relationships observed illustrate undesirable social status (e.g., *"ghosts and guests"* describe an "invisible" social status; *"I'll help"* describes a nonreciprocal relationship; *"The inclusion kid"* suggests differential treatment based on disability), friendships encompassed by the descriptors *"just another kid", "regular friends",* and *"best friends/friends forever"* suggest more equitable and mutually rewarding relationships.

Finally, reports from parents of students who are part of general education classrooms indicate that these placements facilitate friendships outside of school (Bennett et al., 19997). Despite pessimistic assumptions held by some, severity of disability has not been found to preclude the formation of social relations and interactions with typical peers. The observations of Salisbury and Palombaro, however, (1998) merit attention, and are discussed further relative to the next theme.

>   *The potential for social isolation was there, but proactive strategies within a supportive classroom climate seemed sufficient to counterbalance the potentially negative consequences of challenging behaviors and limited expressive capabilities* (pg. 101).

■   ***Teachers play a critical role in facilitating friendships between students with disabilities and their typical peers.***

Within the classroom, opportunities for interaction and relationship-building can be enhanced by purposeful facilitation by teachers. In a longitudinal study of a single student (Kozleski & Jackson, 1993), variation in interaction opportunities within the classroom from year to year was seen as a function of the teacher's approach and involvement in facilitating these interactions. Specific strategies such as the circle of friends process (Forest & Lusthaus, 1989) were effective in encouraging the development of social relationships, and was seen by more than half of the typical students in the class as a unique and special aspect of their fifth grade experience. Only one student in the class perceived this to be a strategy designed to benefit only the student with a disability.

In a qualitative study of 5 inclusive elementary schools, Janney and Snell (1996) sought to identify strategies effectively used by teachers to facilitate inclusion and interaction. They found that teachers made complex judgements in order to know when to encourage interaction and when to "back off". They used typical peers in various ways to assist and promote interaction. Classroom rules about helping changed. Finally, they modeled the message "just another student" in their talk and actions, implicitly conferring classroom membership status to the student with severe disabilities. In contrast to other methods of promoting friendship and support that focus exclusively on the "identified" students, these teachers used whole-classroom strategies based on cooperation and mutual assistance to create a setting in which all students could be supported.

Adults can also interfere with the development of relationships between students with and without disabilities in the regular classroom. Giangreco and colleagues (Giangreco, Edelman, Luiselli & MacFarland, 1997) analyzed interactions between students and instructional assistants in 16 classrooms in 11 schools in four states over two school years. The finding that instructional assistants maintain <u>ongoing</u> physical proximity to students with severe disabilities that they support in the general education classroom has broad implications, but is particularly relevant in the area of peer interaction. Observations and comments by staff suggest that in some cases, the constant proximity of an adult inhibits interaction with peers. When instructional assistants had established good relationships with typical peers, the opposite effect was noted. The potential for adults to disrupt interaction requires further examination. There is enough evidence to suggest this should be looked at closely in inclusive classrooms.

■ *Friendship and membership is facilitated by longitudinal involvement in the classroom and routine activities of the school.*

At least two approaches have been taken to promote interaction and friendship between students with and without disabilities. Early published reports describe special programs or interventions (e.g., special friends) to bring students together, based on the knowledge that contact with people with disabilities positively influences attitudes (Voeltz, 1982). The limitations of this periodic contact outside the ongoing structures and activities of the general education classroom are suggested by two studies. In an early analysis of student interaction in integrated preschools, Guralnick (1981) found that students with mild disabilities were more socially integrated than those with more significant differences. However, these students were members of the same class, while other students were integrated for only select activities. Hanline (1993) commented "It may be that the shared experiences created by full inclusion provide the foundation for more social integration" (pg. 33). Using qualitative methodology, Schnorr (1990) observed and talked with first graders in an effort to understand their perception of a "part time" mainstreamed student. In the eyes of the typical students, this student did not "belong" to the class because he did not share in the school experiences that, for these children, defined what it meant to be in first grade.

More recent efforts to promote friendship are embedded within the context of the ongoing school and classroom routine. These strategies attempt to encourage natural relationships between students and their peers in these shared settings. In a second investigation of the elusive concept of membership and belonging, Schnorr (1997) found that in middle and high school classes, student membership and belonging depends upon developing an affiliation with a subgroup of peers within the class. In her study of students with disabilities in four classes, she observed that some students were successful in connecting with a subgroup, while others were not. Taken together, these studies emphasize the importance of "being there" in order to develop these social connections.

Impact on Students without Disabilities

A frequent concern about the involvement of students with disabilities in general education classroom is that their presence will be detrimental to other students in the class. Three themes that address this issue, as well as the benefits that students derive from this approach to education, characterize the research focused on this population.

■   *The performance of typically-developing students is not compromised by the presence of students with disabilities in their classrooms.*

Many early investigations of the impact of students with disabilities on the developmental progress of typical students were conducted in preschool programs involving students with varying degrees and types of disabilities. Findings of studies with and without the use of a control group consistently demonstrated that the development of typically developing children did not decelerate (e.g., Bricker et al., 1982; Odom et al., 1984) as a function of the diversity of children in the classroom. Among school-aged students, consistent results have been obtained (Sharpe, York & Knight, 1994), although the research is sparse in this area. Measurement issues (i.e., the questionable sensitivity of standardized academic and behavioral measures typically employed by schools) complicate this type of investigation.

Several studies have examined this issue from a different perspective, seeking to investigate concerns that students with disabilities require a disproportionate amount of teacher attention, and therefore take away from the educational opportunities for other students. In the Johnson City School District (Hollowood, Salisbury, Rainforth & Palombaro, 1994/95), an investigation focused on the use of instructional time was implemented, comparing the teacher's use of time in classrooms with and without students with severe disabilities. Results indicated no difference in engagement rates between classrooms, suggesting no negative impact on instructional opportunities. Similar findings are reported by McDonnell et al. (1997) in another direct comparison of classrooms with and without students with severe disabilities.

Examining this issue from yet another perspective, skill acquisition of typical students who are involved in small instructional groups containing a student with a severe disability has been examined by Dugan et al. (1995) and Hunt et al. (1994). In each case, the general education students and the students with disabilities that were part of small cooperative goups demonstrated academic gains. In contrast, mixed results were obtained by O'Connor and Jenkins (1996) in a study focused on cooperative groups comprised of typical students and students with mild disabilities in grades three through six. While some groups were successful, others were not. Factors such as partner selection, teacher monitoring, and the establishment of a cooperative ethic appeared to influence the outcomes. Clearly, structure and support are essential to the success of these arrangements, and more research is needed to clarify critical organizational elements.

Finally, data from at least one study are available to respond to the concern that typical students will model inappropriate behavior exhibited by some students with disabilities. In a year long observational study in an inclusive elementary classroom, Staub and colleagues (Staub et al., 1994) did not find evidence to substantiate this fear.

■   ***Typically developing students derive benefits from their involvement and relationships with students with disabilities.***

Much of the research documenting positive outcomes for typically developing students has been survey research in which students themselves are the respondents (e.g., Helmstetter, Peck & Giangreco, 1994; Kishi & Meyer, 1994; Peck, Donaldson & Pezzoli, 1990). Benefits described by students revolve around several themes, including improvement in self-concept, growth in social cognition, and reduced fear of human differences (Peck, et al., 1990). These results are corroborated in studies based on parental reports of child outcomes (e.g., Ginagreco et al., 1993c; Miller et al., 1992). Furthermore, benefits associated with relationships with peers with disabilities have been found to persist far beyond the time that students are actively involved with each other (Kishi & Meyer, 1994).

In the context of all of these potential benefits, it is equally important to attend to information about the supports that are necessary in order to maxmize the potentially positive outcomes of these experiences. Students participating in a series of focus groups (York & Tunidor, 1995) reported the need for more information about students with disabilities in order to feel more comfortable in these relationships. Similarly, middle and high school students responding to a survey about potential friendships with students with disabilities felt that they should initiate these relationships, but also reported they might not know what to do (Henrickson, Shokoohi-Hekta, Hamre-Nietupski, & Gable, 1996).

■   ***The presence of students with disabilities in the general education classroom provides a catalyst for learning opportunities and experiences that might not otherwise be part of the curriculum.***

The inclusion of students with disabilities in general education classrooms stimulates activities, opportunities, and experiences that might not otherwise occur within the general education classroom. In a review of various program models designed to support students with mild disabilities in regular classrooms, Manset and Semmel (1997) write that the most consistent positive result across program models are gains for non-identified students. This suggests that some of the instructional strategies and organizational approaches typically introduced into the general education setting for the purpose of supporting identified students actually yield academic benefits for a far wider range of students.

Students with disabilities also create the opportunity to engage typical students in dialogues around issues that might otherwise go untouched within the scope and sequence of the curriculum. In the context of providing ongoing accommodations, issues about fairness and equity naturally arise (e.g., *Why does she get to work on that while I have to do this?"*). Qualitative investigations of classrooms in which these issues were actively raised and discussed have been associated with the acquisition of sophisticated social cognition skills by students without disabilities. In one such study (Evans, Salisbury, Palombaro & Goldberg, 1994), even students in kindergarten exhibited highly sophisticated concepts of fairness, and could articulate principles of equal treatment. In this same school, teachers successfully taught elementary-aged students to use a collaborative problem solving process to eliminate barriers to various issues related to the inclusion of students with disabilities (Salisbury, Evans & Palombaro, 1997). Children successfully assumed the role of problem-solver, identifying solutions to address physical, social, academic, and staffing problems associated with students included in their classrooms. While these skills and values may have been learned through other experiences, they were a vital and recurring part of these classrooms as a result of the naturally occurring situations that arose in the course of supporting students with a wide range of skills within the general education setting. In a similar vein, Kozleski and Jackson (1993) report student comments that suggest activities such as Circle of Friends, stimulated by the presence of a student with a disability in the classroom, were viewed as beneficial for many of the students.

A final observation relative to this theme relates to a finding by York and Tunidor (1995), generated in their discussions with typical students. Students reported a willingness to do far more than they were asked to do by adults in initial efforts to include students with disabilities in general education classes. The presence of these students creates opportunities for others to serve in roles or assume responsibilities that were previously not available. Clearly, some are willing to take advantage of these opportunities, and may experience considerable personal growth as a result.

Impact on Parents

While parent perceptions about inclusive services have already been discussed, it is helpful to consider the differing levels of interest and support for inclusion in light of other educational issues of importance to parents. Two themes capture the flavor of this literature.

■   *Parent support for inclusion is positively impacted by actual experience with this approach to education, although experience alone does not shape attitudes.*

Studies have shown that, while not universal, support for inclusion is strong among parents of typical students (Bailey & Winton, 1987; Diamond & LeFurgy, 1994) as well as parents of students with disabilities. One variable positively associated with the level of parent support is current or previous experience in inclusive settings (Miller et al., 1992; Palmer et al., 1998). Another variable associated with differences in attitudes is parent age. Green and Stoneman (1989) found parents of young children with disabilities to hold more positive attitudes toward integration than those of older children (Green & Stoneman, 1989).

Experience with inclusive services is explored in studies from several perspectives. Among parents of students receiving resource room services, Green and Shinn (1994) noted positive responses to questions about regular class placements, but reluctance when asked about their willingness to have their child reintegrated. Parents of students with experience in both settings described by Lowenbraun et al. (1990) gave comparable ratings to resource room and regular class placements once their children were in general education settings, despite their lower ratings for academic progress and self-esteem in resource room programs. Green and Shinn (1994) found parental satisfaction to be related to subjective feelings about teacher attitudes and support rather than data about their child's academic progress. It was, seemingly, this emphasis that enabled them to continue to strongly support pull out services despite an absence of academic gains.

■ *Parents of students with disabilities are looking for positive attitudes, good educational opportunities, and acceptance of their child among educators.*

The previous discussion leads to further consideration of what parents hope to have in a special education placement. In Green and Shinn's (1994) sample, parents clearly valued the relationship between the special educator and their child, and the knowledge that their child is receiving individual attention. While not focused on placement, Giangrego and colleagues (Giangreco, Cloninger, Mueller, Yuan & Ashworth, 1991) interviewed 28 parents of students with dual sensory impairments about the services provided to their children. Responses in this study underscore the importance of the relationship between the family and the teacher. Furthermore, this group of parents expressed strong concerns about program stability, fear about the future, and frustration with the varied and continually changing team of professionals with whom they are involved. They wanted to be heard and consulted when decisions were considered about programmatic changes for their child. This parental advice is particularly helpful to consider in the context of the multiple changes associated with the implementation of any program model.

Impact on Teachers

■ *Although many teachers are initially reluctant about inclusion, they become confident in their abilities with support and experience.*

Studies of the impact of inclusion on teachers have captured their feelings and behavior at different points in their involvement with this instructional model. Initial feelings of uncertainty and resistance were documented by Giangreco et al. (1993b) among 18 teachers asked to include students with severe disabilities for the first time. Similar sentiments are documented in dialogue journals kept by teachers newly involved in a cooperative teaching model (Salend, Johansen, Mumper, Chase, Pike & Dorney, 1997) and in the responses teachers gave in the Wood's (1998) qualitative study. Over time, teachers in the Salend study were able to blend their skills and work effectively as a team. A "transformation" also occurred in the teacher sample described by Giangreco et al. Their comments suggest increased confidence, and a sense of professional growth in terms of their ability to accommodate a more diverse group of students in their classroom as they gain experience with different children. Bennett, DeLuca and Bruns (1997) found a positive relationship between teacher confidence and experience with inclusion.

Resources, time, and training emerge as intervening variables in understanding the varying reactions and success of general educators with inclusion. Teachers who feel adequately supported in their efforts to include students are more likely to report being successful in their efforts (Bennett et al., 1997; Gemmel-Crosby & Hanzlik, 1994; Wolery, Werts, Caldwell, Snyder & Liskowski, 1995). Several studies evaluating the effects of specific training interventions with teachers designed to broaden their instructional repertoire have documented positive results for both teachers and students (Brady, Swank, Taylor & Freiberg, 1992; Wolery, Anthony, Snyder, Werts & Katzenmeyer, 1997).

■ *Support from other teachers is a powerful and necessary resource to empower teachers to problem-solve new instructional challenges.*

The most frequently recommended type of support for general educators who are including students with disabilities in their classroom is some form of collaboration or co-teaching arrangement with special educators (e.g., Friend & Cooke, 1996). These relationships have been found to be associated with periods of uncertainty, as teachers develop new roles and the ability to effectively partner with other teaching personnel (Salend et al., 1997; Wood, 1998). Work by Pugach and Johnson (1995) in promoting peer support between general educators demonstrated that helping teachers to use reflective, structured dialogues to problem-solve and brainstorm challenges that arose in each others' classrooms enabled them to successfully solve 88% of the problemmatic situations they encountered in their classes. While this evidence does not negate the complementary expertise that is blended in inclusive programs when special and general educators collaborate, it does highlight the essential element of problem-solving and support, from whatever source, to enable teachers to feel that solutions to new classroom challenges lie within their reach. A recent report about the use of action research to solve instructional situations associated with inclusion (Salisbury, Wilson, Swartz, Palombaro & Wassel, 1997) reinforces this observation, illustrating another way in which support can be directed to the teacher to discover solutions that are effective and contextually relevant for his or her particular situation.

■   *Facilitating the inclusion of students with disabilities requires the sensitivity to make on-the-spot judgements about the type and amount of support to encourage participation while not interfering with student interactions.*

Observational studies conducted of teachers including students with significant disabilities in general education classes has led to rich descriptions of the strategies they use to facilitate ongoing involvement in general education activities. Janney and Snell (1996) identified at least five different approaches used by teachers to facilitate student involvement, including strategies that are diametrically opposed to each other. For instance, teachers used multiple strategies to actively encourage engagement and interaction, but also purposefully used a "backing off" strategy to allow interaction to occur more naturally. Ferguson et al. (Ferguson, Meyer, Janchild, Juniper & Zingo, 1992) also provide rich description of varied types and levels of support provided by instructional staff, encompassing teaching supports, prosthetic supports, and interventions that assist others in interpreting the actions or intent of a student. These examples highlight the discriminations and judgements that seem to be implied when teaching is described as artistic. They suggest the application of carefully honed observational skills to the diverse instructional landscape that is created when students with very differing abilities are part of general education classrooms. Teachers that were nominated by peers as effective inclusionists described themselves as tolerant, reflective, and flexible, willing to accept responsibility for all students (Olson, Chalmers & Hoover, 1997). Perhaps it is these qualities that contribute to a mind set that stimulates the level of perceptiveness that these descriptions suggest.

Program-Related Outcomes

Issues of the cost-effectiveness of inclusive models have received some attention in the literature. This is a methodologically challenging area to investigate, prompting the caveat that existing evidence should viewed in this light.

■   *These is some evidence to suggest that while start-up costs may initially increase the cost of inclusive services, the costs over time decrease, and are likely to be less than segregated forms of service delivery.*

The costs of implementing an inclusive model in a local school district were compared with the costs of serving students with disabilities in out of district placements (Salisbury & Chambers, 1994). An inclusive model was found to be less costly. Other analyses of cost suggest that there are initial start-up costs associated with inclusion that increase its costs to districts (McLaughlin & Warren, 1994). Over time, however, this is not likely to be the case. In some areas, savings in transportation may actually reduce the costs of providing services in an inclusive manner.

Discussions of this issue underscore the complexity of making cost comparisons due, in large part, to the differences in exactly what costs are reflected in general and special education budgets (McLaughlin & Warren, 1994). A model developed by Halvorsen and colleagues (Halvorsen, Neary, Hunt & Piuma, 1996) attempts to quantify all actual costs of providing instruction, viewing these costs relative to their effects on students in inclusive classrooms. The analysis of effects is not limited to outcomes for students with disabilities. They also consider the "value added" to the general education classroom in terms of the extra services available to non-labeled students as a result of a special educator delivering services within the classroom. While still at the pilot stage, this model provides a more educationally grounded approach to examining the benefit side of a cost/benefit analysis.

Concluding Observations and Future Directions

The philosophy, practices, and expectations associated with inclusive schooling practices continue to evolve as our experience with this approach to education increases. As such, the collective picture of the theoretical and empirical basis for inclusive practices presented in this synthesis is much like a still photograph of something in motion. The feeling of movement is present within a stationary object, creating a picture that is simultaneously clear and fuzzy, depending upon where one's attention is directed. Collectively, these component parts form a picture that communicates progress toward an outcome that is defined differently for each person who sees the picture, based on their particular experiences and interests.

Based on the information and evidence presented in this monograph, clear images of students with a wide range of abilities truly belonging to general education classes can be seen. These classrooms are interactive and stimulating environments, structured around principles that acknowledge and celebrate the inherent diversity in a group of similarly-aged learners. However, there are less-focused images around the edges, accentuated from other vantage points and by some observers. It is possible to make out groups of teachers uncertain of their roles and priorities, parents trying to determine which way to go, and bits and pieces of a complex backdrop of school activities seemingly unconnected to this single classroom. For some, this is the predominant image.

While we have learned much about what it takes to support students with a wide range of abilities in general education classes, our lessons are largely grounded in the realm of special education. Connections to the larger "whole" of the school are not clearly visible from all perspectives. It is the connection of efforts to include students with disabilities to the larger school, district and state level contexts that must be a primary focus of the future as efforts to make schools more inclusive continue. The contextual variables that influence the success of inclusion exist within the general education setting. There is great reason to be optimistic when the exemplary theories and practices of general education are considered. With respect and active acknowledgement of the diversity of the student population, classrooms embracing general education "best practices" provide a desirable and necessary context for inclusion. Udvari-Solner and Thousand (1995) encourage administrators to actively work to dispel the perception of competition between general education reforms and inclusion, showing teachers how these efforts are congruent. These efforts will be supported with research and documented outcomes that demonstrate these beliefs to be true.

Toward this end, future research and demonstration needs to be focused on classroom-wide and building-wide contexts, reflecting an alignment within special education as well as between special and general education. It is important to understand that inclusion works not only for the "target" students or exemplary classrooms, but for the rest of the class and school as well. Efforts to date strongly underscore the importance of collaboration and mutual support between general and special educators, but further examples of how this ideal is realized in the human contexts of schools is necessary. Similarly, a better understanding of the elements and dynamics of the general education setting that make it possible to respond to needs of diverse learners will be important in supporting best practice theory and philosophy with outcome measures that encompass all members of the heterogeneous classroom.

Sapon-Shevin (1994/1995) observed that "an essential component of wide-ranging school reform is a shared agenda: the understanding that fixing the school for some children must mean fixing the school for all children" (pg. 70). The research to date provides ample indication that collective resources, strategies, and creativity of both general and special education is necessary and sufficient to achieve this goal.

References

Adamson, D., Cox, J., & Schuller, J. (1989). Collaboration/consultation: Bridging the gap from resource room to regular classroom. Teacher Education and Special Education, 12(1-2), 52-55.

Adelman, N. E., & Walking-Eagle, K. P. (1997). Teachers, time, and school reform. In A. Hargreaves (Ed.), 1997 ASCD yearbook. Rethinking educational change with heart and mind (pp. 92-110). Alexandria, VA: Association for Supervision and Curriculum Development.

Affleck, J., Madge, S., Adams, A., & Lowenbraun, S. (1988). Integrated classroom versus resource model: Academic viability and effectiveness. Exceptional Children, 54, 339-348.

Alper, L., Fendel, D., Fraser, S., & Resek, D. (1996). Problem-based mathematics -Not just for the college-bound. Educational Leadership, 53(8), 18-21.

Anderson, R. H., & Pavan, B. N. (1993). Nongradedness. Helping it to happen. Lancaster, PA: Technomonic.

Apple, M. W., & Beane, J. A. (1995). Democratic schools. Alexandria, VA: Association of Supervision and Curriculum Development.

Armstrong, T. (1994). Multiple intelligences in the classroom. Alexandria, VA: Association of Supervision and Curriculum Development.

Aronson, E., Blaney, N., Stephan, C., Sikes, J., & Snapp, M. (1978). The jigsaw classroom. Beverly Hills, CA: Sage.

Aspy, D. N., Aspy, C. B., & Quinby, P. M. (1993). What doctors can teach teachers about problem-based learning. Educational Leadership, 50(7), 22-24.

Astuto, T. A., Clark, D. L., Read, A., McGree, K., & Fernandez, L.D.P. (1994). Roots of reform: Challenging the assumption that control change in education. Bloomington, IN: Phi Delta Kappan Foundation.

Bailey, D., & Winton, P. (1987). Stability and change in parents' expectations about mainstreaming. Topics in Early Childhood Special Education, 7(1), 73-88.

Bailey, D., & Winton, P. (1989). Friendship and acquaintance among families in a mainstreamed day care center. Education and Training of the Mentally Retarded, 24, 107-113.

Baker, J. M. (1995a). Inclusion in Virginia: Educational experiences of students with learning disabilities in one elementary school. The Journal of Special Education, 29(2), 116-123.

Baker, J. M. (1995b). Inclusion in Minnesota: Educational experiences of students with learning disabilities in two elementary schools. The Journal of Special Education, 29(2), 133-143.

Baker, J. M. (1995c). Inclusion in Washington: Educational experiences of students with learning disabilities in one elementary school. The Journal of Special Education, 29(2), 155-162.

Baker, J. M., & Zigmond, N. (1990). Are regular education classes equipped to accommodate students with learning disabilities? Exceptional Children, 56, 515-526.

Baker, J. M., & Zigmond, N. (1995). The meaning and practice of inclusion for students with learning disabilities: Themes and implications from the five cases. The Journal of Special Education, 29(2), 163-180.

Ballard, M., Corman, L., Gottlieb, J., & Kauffman, M. J. (1978). Improving the social status of mainstreamed retarded children. Journal of Education Psychology, 69, 605-611.

Barbe, W. B., & Swassing, R. H. (1979). <u>Teaching through modality strengths: Concepts and practices</u>. Columbus, OH: Zaner-Bloser, Inc.

Barth, R. (1990). A personal vision of a good school. <u>Phi Delta Kappan, 71</u>, 512-521.

Bateman, B. (1995). Who, how, and where: Special education's issues in perpetuity. In J. M. Kauffman & D. P. Hallahan (Eds.), <u>The illusion of full inclusion. A comprehensive critique of a current special education bandwagon</u> (pp. 75-90). Austin, TX: Pro-Ed.

Bauwens, J., Hourcade, J. J., & Friend, M. (1989). Cooperative teaching: A model for general and special education integration. <u>Remedial and Special Education, 10</u>, 17-22.

Beninghof, A. M., & Singer, A. L. (1995). <u>Ideas for inclusion. The school administrtator's guide</u>. Longmont, CO: Sopris West.

Bennett, T., DeLuca, D., & Bruns, D. (1997). Putting inclusion into practice: Perspectives of teachers and parents. <u>Exceptional Children, 64</u>(1), 115-131.

Ben-Peretz, M. (1990). <u>The teacher-curriculum encounter: Freeing teachers from the tyranny of texts.</u> New York: State University of New York Press.

Billingsley, F. F., & Kelley, B. (1994). An examination of the acceptability of instructional practices for students with severe disabilities in general education settings. <u>Journal of the Association for Persons with Severe Handicaps, 19</u>(2), 75-83.

Block, J. H. (1980). Promoting excellence through mastery learning. <u>Theory into Practice, 19</u>(1), 66- 74.

Bolanos, P. (1990). Restructuring the curriculum. <u>Principal</u>, 13-14.

Brady, M. P., Shores, R., Gunter, P., McEvoy, M. A., Fox, J. J., & White, C. (1984). Generalization of an adolescent's social interaction behavior via multiple peers in a classroom settings. <u>Journal of the Association for Persons with Severe Handicaps, 9</u>, 278-286.

Brady, M. P., Swank, P. R., Taylor, R. D., & Freiberg, J. (1992). <u>Exceptional Children, 58</u>(6), 530-540.

Bricker, D. D., Bruder, M. B., & Bailey, E. (1982). Developmental integration of preschool children. Analysis and <u>Intervention in Developmental Disabilities, 2</u>, 207-222.

Brinker, R. P. (1985). Interactions between severely mentally retarded students and other students in integrated and segregated public school settings. <u>American Journal of Mental Deficiency, 89</u>, 587- 594.

Brinker, R. P., & Thorpe, M. E. (1984). Integration of severely handicapped students and the proportion of IEP objectives achieved. <u>Exceptional Children, 51</u>, 168-175.

Brinker, R. P., & Thorpe, M. E. (1986). Features of integrated educational ecologies that predict social behavior among severely mentally retarded and nonretarded students. <u>American Journal of Mental Deficiency, 91</u>, 150-159.

Brooks, J. G., & Brooks, M. G. (1993). <u>In search of understanding. The case for constructivist classrooms.</u> Alexandria, VA: Association of Supervision and Curriculum Development.

Brown, L., Ford, A., Nisbet, J., Sweet, M., Donnellan, A., & Gruenewald, L. (1983). Opportunities available when severely handicapped students attend chronological age appropriate regular schools. <u>Journal of the Association for the Severely Handicapped, 8</u>, 16-24.

Brown, L., Long, E., Udvari-Solner, A., Davis, L., VanDeventer, P., Ahlgren, C., Johnson, F., Gruenewald, L., & Jorgensen, J. (1989). The home school: Why students with severe intellectual disabilities must attend the school of their brothers, sisters, friends, and neighbors. Journal of the Association for Persons with Severe Handicaps, 14(1), 1-7.

Brown, L., Rogan, P., Shiraga, B., Zanella, K., Albright, K., Kessler, K., Bryson, F., VanDeventer, P., & Loomis, R. (1987). A vocational followup evaluation of the 1984 to 1986 Madison Metropolitan School District graduates with severe intellectual disabilities (Monograph). Seattle, WA: The Association for Persons with Severe Handicaps.

Brubacher, J. W., Case, C. W., & Reagan, T. G. (1994). Becoming a reflective educator. How to build a culture of inquiry in the schools. Thousand Oaks, CA: Corwin Press.

Bruininks, V. L. (1978). Actual and perceived peer status of learning-disabled students in mainstream programs. Journal of Special Education, 12, 51-58.

Bryan, T. S. (1974). Peer popularity of learning disabled children. Journal of Learning Disabilities, 7, 621-625.

Bryan, T. S. (1978). Peer popularity of learning disabled children: A replication. Journal of Learning Disabilities, 9, 307-311.

Buber, M. (1965). Between man and man. Trans. Ronald Gregor Smith. New York: Macmillan.

Burke, J. (1993). Tackling society's problems in English class. Educational Leadership, 50(7), 16-18.

California Research Institute (1992, Spring). Educational practices in integrated settings associated with positive student outcomes. Strategies on the Integration of Students with Severe Disabilities, 3(3), 1, 10.

Canady, R. L., & Rettig, M. D. (1995). Block scheduling. A catalyst for change in high schools. Princeton, NJ: Eye on Education.

Carr, M. N. (1995). A mother's thoughts on inclusion. In J. M. Kauffman & D. P. Hallahan (Eds.), The illusion of full inclusion. A comprehensive critique of a current special education bandwagon (pp. 263-267). Austin, TX: Pro-Ed.

Cawaleti, G. (1994). High school restructuring: A national study. Arlington, VA: Educational Research Service.

Choate, J. S. (Ed). (1993). Successful mainstreaming. Proven ways to detect and correct special needs. Boston: Allyn & Bacon.

Charney, R. S. (1991). Teaching children to care. Management in the responsive classroom. Greenfield, MA: Northeast Foundation for Children.

Charney, R. S. (1997). Habits of goodness. Case studies in the social curriculum. Greenfield, MA: Northeast Foundation for Children.

Cheney, D., & Harvey, V. S. (1994). From segregation to inclusion: One district's program changes for students with emotional/behavioral disorders. Education and Treatment of Children, 17, 332- 346.

Child Development Project (1994). At home in our schools: A guide to schoolwide activities that build community. Oakland, CA: Developmental Studies Center.

Choate, J. S. (1993). Successful mainstreaming. Proven ways to detect and correct special needs. Boston, MA: Allyn & Bacon.

Christ, G. M. (1995). Curriculums with real-world connection. Educational Leadership, 52(8), 32-35.

Clark, F. L., Deshler, D. D., Schumaker, J. B., & Alley, G. R. (1984). Visual imagery and self-questioning: Strategies to improve comprehension of written materials. Journal of Learning Disabilities, 17(3), 145-149.

Clyde K. and Sheila K. v. Puyallup School District, 21 IDELR 664 (Wash. 1996).

Coates, R. D. (1989). The Regular Education Initiative and opinions of regular classroom teachers. Journal of Learning Disabilities, 22, 532-536.

Cohen, E. G. (1994). Designing groupwork (Second edition). New York: Teachers College Press.

Cohen, J. (1986). Theoretical considerations of peer tutoring. Psychology in the Schools, 23, 175- 186.

Cohen, P. A., Kulik, J. A., & Kulik, C. C. (1982). Educational outcomes of tutoring. American Educational Research Journal, 19, 237-248.

Cole, D. A., & Meyer, L. H. (1991). Social integration and severe disabilities: A longitudinal analysis of child outcomes. Journal of Special Education, 25, 340-351.

Conoley, J. C., & Conoley, C. W. (1982). School consultation: A guide to practice and training. New York: Pergamon Press.

Consortium on Inclusive Schooling Practices. (1996, December). A framework for evaluating state and local policies for inclusion. Issue Brief, 1-12.

Cooke, T. P., Ruskus, J. A., Apolloni, T., & Peck, C. A. (1981). Handicapped preschool children in the mainstream: Background, outcomes, and clinical suggestions. Topics in Early Childhood Special Education, 1(1), 78-83.

Cooper, H. M. (1989). Integrating research. A guide for literature reviews (Second edition). Newbury Park: Sage Publications.

Cosden, M. A., & Haring, T. G. (1992). Cooperative learning in the classroom: Contingencies, group interactions, and students with special needs. Journal of Behavioral Education, 2(1), 53-71.

Crane, S. J., & Iwanicki, E. F. (1986). Perceived role conflict, role ambiguity, and burnout among special education teachers. Remedial and Special Education, 724-31.

Cross, G., & Villa, R. (1992). The Winooski school system: An evolutionary perspective of a school restructuring for diversity. In R. Villa, J. Thousand, W. Stainback, & S. Stainback (Eds.), Restructuring for caring and effective education: An administrative guide to creating heterogeneous schools (pp. 219-237). Baltimore: Paul H. Brookes.

Crowley, E. . (1993). A qualitative analysis of mainstreamed behaviorally disordered aggressive adolescents' perceptions of helpful and unhelpful teacher attitudes and behaviors. Exceptionality, 4(3), 131-151.

Cuban, L. (1988a). Why do some reforms persist? Educational Administration Quarterly, 24(3), 329- 335.

Cuban, L. (1988b). A fundamental puzzle of school reform. Phi Delta Kappan, 70(5), 341-344.

Cuban, L. (1989). The 'at-risk' label and the problem of urban school reform. Phi Delta Kappan, 70, 780-784, 799-801.

Cuban, L. (1996). Myths about changing schools and the case of special education. Remedial and Special Education, 17(2), 75-82.

Curwin, R. L. (1993). The healing power of altruism. Educational Leadership, 51(3), 36-39.

Dalton, J., & Watson, M. (1997). Among friends. Oakland, CA: Developmental Studies Center.

Daniel R. R. v. State Board of Education, 874 F.2d 1036 (5th Cir. 1989).

Danielson, C. (1995). Whither standardized assessment? In A. L. Costa & B. Kallick (Eds.), Assessment in the learning organization (pp. 84-90). Alexandria, VA: Association of Supervision and Curriculum Development.

Darling-Hammond, L. (1993). Reframing the school reform agenda. Phi Delta Kappan, 74, 753-761.

Darling-Hammond, L., Ancess, J., & Falk, B. (1995). Authentic assessment in action. Studies of schools and students at work. New York: Teachers College Press.

Dawson, M. M. (1987). Beyond ability grouping: A review of the effectiveness of ability grouping and its alternatives. School Psychology Review, 16, 348-369.

DeBoer, A. L. (1986). The art of consulting. Chicago: Arcturus.

Deshler, D. D., & Schumaker, J. B. (1986). Learning strategies: An instructional alternative for low-achieving adolescents. Exceptional Children, 52(6), 583-590.

Devoney, C., Guralnick, M. J., & Rubin, H. (1974). Integrating handicapped and non-handicapped preschool children: Effects on social play. Childhood Education, 50, 360-364.

DeVries, D., Slavin, R., Fennessey, G., Edwards, K., & Lombardo, M. (1980). Teams-games- tournament: The team learning approach. Englewood Cliffs, NJ: Educational Technology Publications.

Dewey, J. (1938). Experience and education. New York: Macmillan.

Dewey, J. (1943). The child and the curriculum and the school and the society. Chicago: University of Chicago Press.

D.F. v. Western Sch. Corp., 23 IDELR 1121 (Ind. 1996).

Diamond, K. E., & LeFurgy, W. G. (1994). Attitudes of parents of preschool children toward integration. Early Education and Development, 5(1), 69-77.

Donaldson, J. (1980). Changing attitudes toward handicapped persons: A review and analysis of research. Exceptional Children, 46(7), 504-513.

Dugan, E., Kamps, D., Leonard, B., Watkins, N., Rehinberger, A., & Stackhaus, J. (1995). Effects of cooperative learning groups during social studies for students with autism and fourth-grade peers. Journal of Applied Behavior Analysis, 28, 175-188.

Dunn, L. M. (1968). Special education for the mildly retarded - Is much of it justifiable? Exceptional Children, 35, 5-22.

Dunn, R. (1996). How to implement and supervise a learning styles program. Alexandria, VA: Association of Supervision and Curriculum Development.

Dunn, R., & Dunn, K. (1975). Educator's self-teaching guide to individualizing instructional programs. New York: Parker Publishing Company.

Dunn, R., Grigg, S. A., Olson, J., Gorman, B., & Beasley, M. (1995). A meta-analytic validation of the Dunn and Dunn Research Learning Styles Model. Journal of Educational Research, 88, 6, 353-361.

Edwards, L. L. (1980). Curriculum modification as a strategy for helping regular classroom behavior-disordered students. Focus on Exceptional Children, 12(8), 1-11.

Eggbrecht, J., Dagenais, R., Dosch, D., Merczak, N. J., Park, M. N., Styer, S. C., & Workman, D. (1996). Reconnecting the sciences. Educational Leadership, 53(8), 4-8.

Eichinger, J. (1990). Goal structure effects on social interaction: Nondisabled and disabled elementary students. Exceptional Children, 56, 408-417.

English, K., Goldstein, H., Shafer, K., & Kaczmarek, L. (1997). Promoting interactions among preschoolers with and without disabilities: Effects of a buddy skill-training program. Exceptional Children, 63(2), 229-244.

Erwin, E. J., & Sodak, L. C. (1995). I never knew I could stand up to the system: Families' perspectives on pursuing inclusive education. Journal of the Association for Persons with Severe Handicaps, 20(2), 136-146.

Evans, I. M., Salisbury, C. L., Palombaro, M. M., Berryman, J., & Hollowood, T. M. (1992). Peer interactions and social acceptance of elementary-age children with severe disabilities in an inclusive school. Journal of the Association for Persons with Severe Handicaps, 17(4), 205-212.

Evans, I. M., Salisbury, C., Palombaro, M., & Goldberg, J. S. (1994). Children's perception of fairness in classroom and interpersonal situations involving peers with severe disabilities. Journal of the Association for Persons with Severe Handicaps, 19(4), 326-332.

Falvey, M., Givner, C. C., & Kimm, C. (1995). What is an inclusive school? In R. A. Villa & J. S. Thousand (Eds.), Creating an inclusive school (pp. 1-12). Alexandria, Va: Association for Supervision and Curriculum Development.

Faught, K. K., Balleweg, B. J., Crow, R. E., & van den Pol, R. A. (1983). An analysis of social behaviors among handicapped and nonhandicapped preschool children. Education and Training of the Mentally Retarded, 18(3), 210-214.

Ferguson, D. L., Meyer, G., Janchild, L., Juniper, L., & Zingo, J. (1992). Figuring out what to do with the grownups: How teachers make inclusion "work" for students with disabilities. Journal of the Association for Persons with Severe Handicaps, 17(4), 218-226.

Florida Department of Education. (1989). Evaluating effectiveness, usefulness, practicalitiy of cooperative consultation - 1987-1988 pilot study in Florida secondary schools (Research Report No. 10). Tallahassee, FL: Author.

Florida Department of Education. (1990). Cooperative consultation regional training 1989-1990 (Research Report No. 12). Tallahassee, FL: Author.

Forest, M., & Lusthaus, E. (1989). Circles and maps: Promoting educational equality for all students. In S. Stainback, W. Stainback, & M. Forest (Eds.), Educating all students in the mainstream of regular education (pp. 43-58). Baltimore: Paul H. Brookes.

Fox, N. E., & Ysseldyke, J. E. (1997). Implementing inclusion at the middle school level: Lessons from a negative example. Exceptional Children, 64(1), 81-98.

Friend, M. (1984). Consultation skills for resource teachers. Learning Disabilities Quarterly, 7, 246-250.

Friend, M. (1988). Putting consultation into context: Historical and contemporary perspectives. Remedial and Special Education, 9(6), 7-13.

Friend, M., & Cook, L. (1990). Collaboration as a predictor for success in school reform. Journal of Educational and Psychological Consultation, 1(1), 69-86.

Friend, M., & Cook, L. (1996). Interactions. Collaboration skills for school professionals (Second edition). White Plains, NY: Longman.

Fryxell, D., & Kennedy, C. H. (1995). Placement along the continuum of services and its impact on students' social relationships. Journal of the Association for Persons with Severe Handicaps, 20, 259-269.

Fuchs, D., & Fuchs, L. S. (1994). Inclusive schools movement and the radicalization of special education reform. Exceptional Children, 60, 294-309.

Fuchs, D., Fuchs, L. S., Bahr, M. W., Fernstrom, P., & Stecker, P. M. (1990). Prereferral intervention: A prescriptive approach. Exceptional Children, 56(6), 493-513.

Fuchs, L. S., Fuchs, D., & Bishop, N. (1992). Instructional adaptation for students at risk for academic failure. Journal of Educational Research, 86, 70-84.

Fuchs, L. S., Fuchs, D., Hamlett, C. L., Phillips, N. B., & Karns, K. (1995). General educators' specialized adaptation for students with learning disabilities. Exceptional Children, 61(5), 440-459.

Fullan, M. (1993). Change forces: Probing the depths of educational reform. New York: Falmer Press.

Fullan, M., & Hargreaves, A. (1996). What's worth fighting for in your school New York: Teachers College Press.

Fullan, M., & Miles, M. B. (1992). Getting reform right: What works and what doesn't. Phi Delta Kappan, 73, 745-752.

Fullan, M. G., with Stiegelbauer, S. (1991). The new meaning of educational change. New York: Teachers College Press.

Gallagher, J. (1995). The pull of societal forces on special education. In J. M. Kauffman & D. P. Hallahan (Eds.), The illusion of full inclusion. A comprehensive critique of a current special education bandwagon (pp. 91-102). Austin, TX: Pro-Ed.

Gamoran, A. (1992). Synthesis of research: Is ability grouping equitable? Educational Leadership, 50(2), 11-17.

Gans, K. D. (1985). Regular and special educators. Teacher Education and Special Education, 8(4), 188-189.

Gardner, H. (1983). Frames of mind: The theory of multiple intelligences. New York: Basic Books.

Gemmell-Crosby, S., & Hanzlik, J. R. (1994). Preschool teachers' perceptions of including children with disabilities. Educational and Training in Mental Retardation and Developmental Disabilities, 29(4), 279-290.

Gerber, M. M. (1995). Inclusion at the high-water mark? Some thoughts on Zigmond and Baker's case studies of inclusive educational programs. The Journal of Special Education, 29(2), 181-191.

Giangreco, M., Cloninger, C., Dennis, R., & Edelman, S. (1995). Problem-solving methods to facilitate inclusive education. In J. S. Thousand, R. A. Villa, & A. I. Nevin (Eds.), Creativity and collaborative learning. A practical gluide to empowering students and teachers (pp. 321-346). Baltimore: Paul Brookes.

Giangreco, M., Cloninger, C., & Iverson, V. (1993a). Choosing options and accommodations for children (COACH): A guide to planning inclusive education. Baltimore: Paul H. Brookes.

Giangreco, M., Cloninger, C., Mueller, P., Yuan, S., & Ashwroth, S. (1991). Perspectives of parents whose children have dual sensory impairments. Journal of the Association for Persons with Severe Handicaps, 16, 14-24.

Giangreco, M. R., Dennis, R., Cloninger, C., Edelman, S., & Schattman, R. (1993b). "I've counted Jon": Transformational experiences of teachers educating students with disabilities. Exceptional Children, 59(4), 359-373.

Giangreco, M., Edelman, S., Cloninger, C., & Dennis, R. (1993c). My child has a classmate with severe disabilities: What parents of nondisabled children think about full inclusion. Developmental Disabilities Bulletin, 21(1), 77-91.

Giangreco, M., Edelman, S. W., Luiselli, T. E., & MacFarland, S. Z. (1997). Helping or hovering? Effects of instructional assistant proximity on students with disabilities. Exceptional Children, 64(1), 7-18.

Glasser, W. (1990). The quality school. New York: Harper Collins.

Goldstein, M., & Wickstrom, S. (1986). Peer intervention effects on communicative interactions among handicapped and nonhandicapped preschoolers. Journal of Applied Behavior Analysis, 19, 209- 214.

Gollnick, D. M. (1980). Multicultural education. Viewpoints in Teaching and Learning, 56, 1-17.

Goodlad, J. (1982). Toward a vision of the 'educative community'. Remarks at the National Community Education Association Convention, Atlanta, Georgia.

Goodlad, J. (1984). A place called school. New York: McGraw-Hill.

Goodland, J. I., & Field, S. (1993). Teachers for renewing schools. In J. I. Goodland & T. C. Lovitt (Eds.), Integrating general and special education (pp. 229-252). New York: Merrill.

Green, S. K., & Shinn, M. R. (1994). Parent attitudes about special education and reintegration: What is the role of student outcomes? Exceptional Children, 61(3), 269-281.

Green, A., & Stoneman, Z. (1989). Attitudes of mothers and fathers of nonhandicapped children. Journal of Early Intervention, 13(4), 292-304.

Greer V. Rome City School District, 950 F.2d 688 (11th Cir. 1991).

Gregorc, A. (1982). An adult's guide to style. Maynard, MA: Gabriel Systems, Inc.

Gresham, F. M. (1981). Social skills training with handicapped children: A review. Review of Educational Research, 51(1), 139-176.

Gresham, F. M., & Kendall, G. K. (1987). School consultation research: Methodological critique and future research directions. School Psychology Review, 6, 306-316.

Guild, P. B., & Garger, S. (1985). Marching to different drummers. Alexandria, VA: Association for Supervision and Curriculum Development.

Guralnick, M. (1980). Social interaction among preschool children. Exceptional Children, 46, 248-253.

Guralnick, M. (1981). The efficacy of integrating handicapped children in early childhood settings: Research implications. Topics in Early Childhood Education, 1(1), 57-71.

Guralnick, M. J., Connor, R. T., & Hammond, M. (1995). Parent perspectives of peer relationships and friendships in integrated and specialized program. American Journal on Mental Retardation, 99, 457-476.

Guralnick, M., & Groom, J. M. (1988). Peer interactions in mainstreamed and specialized classrooms: A comparative analysis. Exceptional Children, 54(5), 415-425.

Halvorsen, A., Neary, T., Hunt, P., & Piuma, C. (1996). A model for evaluating the cost-effectiveness of inclusive and special classes. Manuscript submitted for publication. Hayward, CA: PEERS Project, California State University, Hayward.

Hamre-Nietupski, S. (1993). How much time should be spent on skill instruction and friendship development? Preferences of parents of students with moderate, severe, or profound disabilities on facilitating friendships between their students and nondisabled peers. Educational and Training in Mental Retardation, 28, 220-231.

Hamre-Nietupski, S., Hendrickson, J., Nietupski, J., & Sasso, G. (1993). Perceptions of teachers of students with moderate, severe, or profound disabilities on facilitating friendships between their students and nondisabled peers. Educational and Training in Mental Retardation, 28, 111-117.

Hamre-Nietupski, S., Hendrickson, J., Nietupski, J., & Shokoohi-Hekta, M. (1994). Regular educators' perceptions of facilitating friendships of students with moderate, severe, or profound disabilities with nondisabled peers. Educational and Training in Mental Retardation, 29(2), 102-117.

Hamre-Nietupski, S., Nietupski, J., & Strathe, M. (1992). Functional life skills, academic skills, and friendship/social relationship development: What do parents of students with moderate/severe/profound disabilities value? Journal of the Association for Persons with Severe Handicaps, 17(1), 53-58.

Hanley, E. M., & Everitt, J. W. (1977). Analysis of special education services in Vermont schools and homes provided through inservice teacher training programs conducted by consulting teachers. Burlington, VT: University of Vermont, Department of Special Education, Social Work and Social Services.

Hanline, M. F. (1993). Inclusion of preschoolers with profound disabilities: An analysis of children's interactions. Journal of the Association for Persons with Severe Handicaps, 18(1), 28-35.

Hargreaves, A. (1994). Changing teachers, changing times. Teachers' work and culture in the postmodern age. New York: Teachers College Press.

Hargreaves, A. (1997a). Introduction. In A. Hargreaves (Ed.), 1997 ASCD yearbook. Rethinking educational change with heart and mind (pp. vii-xv). Alexandria, VA: Association of Supervision and Curriculum Development.

Hargreaves, A. (1997b). Rethinking educational change: Going deeper and wider in the quest for success. In A. Hargreaves (Ed.), 1997 ASCD yearbook. Rethinking educational change with heart and mind (pp. 1-26). Alexandria, VA: Association of Supervision and Curriculum Development.

Hargreaves, A., Earl, L., & Ryan, J. (1996). Schooling for change. London/New York: Falmer Press.

Harper, G. F., Maheady, L., & Mallette, B. (1994). The power of peer-mediated instruction. How and why it promotes academic success for all students. In J. S. Thousand, R. A. Villa, & A. I. Nevin (Eds.), Creativity and collaborative learning. A practical guide to empowering students and teachers (pp. 229-241). Baltimore: Paul H. Brookes.

Hasazi, S. B., Gordon, L. R., & Roe, C. A. (1985). Factors associated with the employment status of handicapped youth exiting high school from 1979 to 1983. Exceptional Children, 51(6), 455- 469.

Helmstetter, E., Peck, C. A., & Giangreco, M. F. (1994). Outcomes of interactions with peers with moderate or severe disabilities: A statewide survey of high school students. Journal of the Association for Persons with Severe Handicaps, 19(4), 263-276.

Hendrickson, J. M., Shokoohi-Hekta, M., Hamre-Nietupski, S., & Gable, R. A. (1996). Middle and high school students' perceptions on being friends with peers with severe disabilities. Exceptional Children, 63(1), 19-28.

Heron, E., & Jorgensen, C. M. (1995). Addressing learning differences right from the start. Educational Leadership, 54(4), 56-58.

Hodgin, J., & Wooliscroft, C. N. (1997). Eric learns to read: Learning styles at work. Educational Leadership, 54(6), 43-45.

Hollowood, T. M., Salisbury, C. L., Rainforth, B., & Palombaro, M. M. (1994/1995). Use of instructional time in classrooms serving students with and without severe disabilities. Exceptional Children, 61(3), 242-253.

Holmes, C. T., & Matthews, K. M. (1984). The effects of nonpromotion on elementary and junior high pupils: A meta-analysis. Review of Educational Research, 54, 225-236.

Hopfenberg, W. S., & Levin, H. M. (1993). The accelerated schools resource guide. San Francisco: Jossey-Bass.

Hord, S. M., Rutherford, W. L., Huling-Austin, L., & Hall, G. E. (1987). Taking charge of change. Alexandria, VA: Association of Supervision and Curriculum Development.

Horne, M. D. (1983). Attitudes of elementary classroom teachers toward mainstreaming. The Exceptional Child, 30, 93-97.

Houck, C. K., & Rogers, C. J. (1994). The special/general education integration initiative for students with specific learning disabilities: A "snapshot" of program change. Journal of Learning Disabilities, 27, 435-453.

Howard, M. B. (1993). Service learning: Character education applied. Educational Leadership, 51(3), 42-43.

Hudson v. Bloomfield Hills School District, 23 IDELR 612 (E.D. Mich. 1995).

Huefner, D. S. (1988). The consulting teacher model: Risks and opportunities. Exceptional Children, 54, 403-424.

Hunt, P., Alwell, M., Farron-Davis, F., & Goetz, L. (1996). Creating socially supportive environments for fully included students who experience multiple disabilities. Journal of the Association for Persons with Severe Handicaps, 21(2), 53-71.

Hunt, P., & Farron-Davis, F. (1992). A preliminary investigation of IEP quality and content associated with placement in general education versus special education classes. Journal of the Association for Persons with Severe Handicaps, 17, 247-253.

Hunt, P., Farron-Davis, F., Beckstead, S., Curtis, D., & Goetz, L. (1994). Evaluating the effects of placement of students with severe disabilities in general education versus special classes. Journal of the Association for Persons with Severe Handicaps, 19(3), 200-214.

Hunt, P., & Goetz, L. (1997). Research on inclusive educational programs, practices, and outcomes for students with severe disabilities. Journal of Special Education, 31(1), 3-29.

Hunt, P., Goetz, L., & Anderson, J. (1986). The quality of IEP objectives associated with placement on integrated vs. segregated school sites. Journal of the Association for Persons with Severe Handicaps, 11, 125-130.

Hunt, P., Staub, D., Alwell, M., & Goetz, L. (1994). Achievement by all students within the context of cooperative learning groups. Journal of the Association for Persons with Severe Handicaps, 19(4), 290-301.

Idol, L., Nevin, A., & Paolucci-Whitcomb, P. (1994). Collaborative consultation (second edition). Austin, TX: Pro-Ed.

Idol, L., & West, J. F. (1987). Consultation in special education (Part II): Training and practice. Journal of Learning Disabilities, 20, 474-497.

Idol-Maestas, L. (1983). Special educator's consultation handbook. Rockville, MD: Aspen.

Idol-Maestas, L., & Jackson, C. (1983). An evaluation of the consultation process. In L. Idol-Maestas (Ed.), Special educator's consultation handbook (pp. 17-19). Rockville, MD: Aspen.

Idol-Maestas, L., & Ritter, S. (1985). A follow up study of resource/consulting teachers: Factors that facilitate and inhibit teacher consultation. Teacher Education and Special Education, 8, 121-131.

Janney, R. E., & Snell, M. E. (1996). How teachers use peer interactions to include students with moderate and severe disabilities in elementary general education classes. Journal of the Association for Persons with Severe Handicaps, 21(2), 72-80.

Janney, R. E., Snell, M. E., Beers, M. K., & Raynes, M. (1995). Integrating students with moderate and severe disabilities into general education classes. Exceptional Children, 61(5), 425-439.

Jenkins, J. R., & Heinen, A. (1989). Students' preferences for service delivery: Pull-out, in-class, or integrated models. Exceptional Children, 55(6), 516-523.

Jenkins, J. R., Odom, S. L., & Speltz, M. L. (1989). Effects of social integration on preschool children with handicaps. Exceptional Children, 55(5), 420-428.

Johnson, D. W., & Johnson, R. T. (1980). Integrating handicapped students into the mainstream. Exceptional Children, 47, 90-98.

Johnson, D. W., & Johnson, R. T. (1981a). The integration of the handicapped into the regular classroom: Effects of cooperative and individualistic instruction. Contemporary Educational Psychology, 6, 344-353.

Johnson, D. W., & Johnson, R. T. (1984). Building acceptance of differences between handicapped and nonhandicapped students: The effects of cooperative and individualistic instruction. The Journal of Social Psychology, 122, 257-267.

Johnson, D. W., & Johnson, R. T. (1986). Mainstreaming and cooperative learning strategies. Exceptional Children, 52, 553-561.

Johnson, D. W., & Johnson, R. T. (1989a). Cooperation and competition: Theory and research. Edina, MN: Interaction Books.

Johnson, D. W., & Johnson, R. T. (1989b). Leading the cooperative school. Edina, MN: Interaction Books.

Johnson, D. W., & Johnson, R. T. (1991). Learning together and alone. Cooperative, competitive, and individualistic learning (Third edition). Englewood Cliffs, NJ: Prentice Hall.

Johnson, D. W., Johnson, R. T., & Anderson, D. (1983). Social interdependence and classroom climate. Journal of Psychology, 114, 135-142.

Johnson, D. W., Johnson, R. T., & Maruyama, G. (1983). Interdependence and interpersonal attraction among heterogeneous and homogeneous individuals: A theoretical formulation and a meta analysis of the research. Review of Educational Research, 53, 5-54.

Johnson, D. W., Johnson, R., Tiffany, M., & Zaidman, B. (1983). Are low achievers disliked in a cooperative situation? A test of rival theories in a mixed ethnic situation. Contemporary Educational Psychology, 8, 189-200.

Johnson, D. W., Johnson, R. T., Warring, D., & Maruyama, G. (1986). Different cooperative learning procedures and cross-handicap relationships. Exceptional Children, 53(3), 247-252.

Johnson, R. T., & Johnson, D. W. (1981b). Building friendships between handicapped and nonhandicapped students: Effects of cooperative vs. individualistic instruction. American Educational Research Journal, 18(4), 415-423.

Johnson, L. J., Pugach, M. C., & Hammitte, D. (1988). Barriers to effective special education consultation. Remedial and Special Education, 9(6), 41-47.

Jolly, A. C., Test, D. W., & Spooner, F. (1993). Using badges to increase initiations of children with severe disabilities in a play setting. Journal of the Association for Persons with Severe Handicaps, 18(1), 46-51.

Jorgensen, C. M. (1996). Designing inclusive curricula right from the start: Practical strategies and examples for the high school classroom. In S. Stainback & W. Stainback (Eds.), Inclusion. A guide for educators (pp. 221-236). Baltimore: Paul H. Brookes.

Jorgensen, C. M. (1995). Essential questions - inclusive answers. Educational Leadership, 54(4), 52- 55.

Jorgensen, C. M., & Fried, R. L. (1994, Spring). Merging school restructuring and inclusive education: An essential partnership to achieve equity and excellence. Equity and Excellence, 2, 10-16.

Jung, C. (1971). Psychological types. Princeton, NJ: Princeton University Press (originally published in 1982).

Kagan, S. (1985). Cooperative learning. Mission-Viejo, CA: Resources for Teachers.

Karge, B. D., McClure, M., & Patton, P. L. (1995). The success of collaboration resource programs for students with disabilities in Grades 6 through 8. Remedial and Special Education, 16(2), 79-89.

Kari H. v. Franklin S.S.D., 23 IDELR 538 (M.D. Tenn. 1995).

Kaskinen-Chapman, A. (1992). Saline Area Schools and inclusive community concepts. In R. Villa, J. Thousand, W. Stainback, & S. Stainback (Eds.), Restructuring for caring and effective education: An administrative guide to creating heterogeneous schools (pp. 169-185). Baltimore: Paul H. Brookes.

Kasten, W., & Clarke, B. (1993). The multi-age classroom: A family of learners. Katonah, NY: Richard C. Owen.

Katsiyannis, A., Conderman, G., & Franks, D. J. (1995). State practices on inclusion. Remedial and Special Education, 16, 279-287.

Kauffman, J. M., & Hallahan, D. P. (1995). The illusion of full inclusion. A comprehensive critique of a current special education bandwagon. Austin, TX: Pro-ed.

Keirsey, D., & Bates, M. (1978). Please understand me. Character and temperament types. Del Mar, CA: Prometheus, Nemesis.

Kennedy, C. H., Shukla, S., & Fryxell, D. (1997). Comparing the effects of educational placement on the social relationships of intermediate school students with severe disabilities. Exceptional Children, 64(1), 31-48.

Kishi, G. S., & Meyer, L. H. (1994). What children report and remember: A six-year follow-up of the effects of social contact between peers with and without severe disabilities. Journal of the Association for Persons with Severe Handicaps, 19(4), 277-289.

Knight, M. F., Meyers, H. W., Paolucci-Whitcomb, P., Hasazi, S. E., & Nevin, A. (1981). A four-year evaluation of consulting teacher service. Behavioral Disorders, 62, 92-100.

Koba, S. B. (1996). Narrowing the achievement gap in science. Educational Leadership, 53(8), 14-17.

Kohn, A. (1991). Caring kids. The role of the schools. Phi Delta Kappan, 72, 496-506.

Kohn, A. (1992). No contest: The case against competition. Houghton Mifflin.

Kohn, A. (1996). What to look for in a classroom. Educational Leadership, 54(1), 54-55.

Kolb, D.(1976). Learning style inventory. Boston: McGer & Company.

Kozleski, E. B., & Jackson, L. (1993). Taylor's story: Full inclusion in her neighborhood elementary school. Exceptionality, 4(3), 153-175.

Kratochwill, T. R., & Van Someren, K. R. (1985). Barriers to treatment success in behavioral consultation: Current limitations and future directions. Journal of School Psychology, 24, 225- 239.

Kreisman, S., Knoll, M., & Melchior, T. (1995). Toward more authentic assessment. In A. L. Costa & B. Kallick (Eds.), Assessment in the learning organization (pp. 114-138). Alexandria, VA: Association of Supervision and Curriculum Development.

Kunc, N. (1992). The need to belong: Rediscovering Maslow's hierarchy of needs. In R. A. Villa, J. S. Thousand, W. Stainback & S. Stainback (Eds.), Restructuring for caring and effective education: An administrative guide to creating heterogeneous schools (pp. 25-40). Baltimore: Paul H. Brookes.

Lantieri, L., & Patti, J. (1996). The road to peace in our schools. Educational Leadership, 55(1), 84- 85.

Lew, M., Mesch, D., Johnson, D. W., & Johnson, R. (1986). Components of cooperative learning: Effects of collaborative skills and academic group contingencies on achievement and mainstreaming. Contemporary Educational Psychology, 11, 229-239.

Lewis, C. C., Schaps, E., & Watson, M. S. (1996). The caring classroom's academic edge. Educational Leadership, 54(1), 16-21.

Lieberman, A. (Ed.) (1995). The work of restructuring schools. Building from the ground up. New York: Teachers College Press.

Lilly, M. S. (1987). Lack of focus on special education in literature on educational reform. Exceptional Children, 53(4), 325-326.

Lipsky, D. K., & Gartner, A. (1996). Inclusion, school restructuring, and the remaking of American society. Harvard Educational Review, 66(4), 762-796.

Lipsky, D. K., & Gartner, A. (1997). Inclusion and school reform. Transforming America's classrooms. Baltimore: Paul H. Brookes.

Lipton, D. (1994). The "full inclusion" court cases: 1989-1994. National Center on Educational Restructuring and Inclusion Bulletin, 1(2), 108.

Logan, K. R., Bakeman, R., & Keefe, E. B. (1997). Effects of instructional variables on engaged behavior of students with disabilities in general education classrooms. Exceptional Children, 63(4), 481-498.

Louis, K. S., & Miles, M. (1990). Improving the urban high school: What works and why. New York: Teachers College Press.

Lowenbraun, S., Madge, S., & Affleck, J. (1990). Parental satisfaction with integrated class placements of special education and general education students. Remedial and Special Education, 11(4), 37-40.

Lyman, F. T. (1992). Think-pair-share, thinktrix, thinklinks, and weird facts. Interactive system for cooperative thinking. In N. Davidson & T. Worsham (Eds.), Enhancing thinking through cooperative learning (pp. 169-181). New York: Teachers College Press.

MacMillan, D. L., Gresham, F. M., & Forness, S. R. (1996). Full inclusion: An empirical perspective. Behavioral Disorders, 21(2), 145-159.

MacMillan, D. L., Semmel, M. I., & Gerber, M. M. (1995). The social context: Then and now. In J. M. Kauffman & D. P. Hallahan (Eds.), The illusion of full inclusion. A comprehensive critique of a current special education bandwagon (pp. 19-38). Austin, TX: Pro-Ed.

Madden, N. A., & Slavin, R. E. (1983a). Effects of cooperative learning on the social acceptance of mainstreamed academically handicapped students. Journal of Special Education, 17, 171-182.

Madden, N. A., & Slavin, R. E. (1983b). Mainstreaming students with mild handicaps: Academic and social outcomes. Review of Educational Research, 53, 519-569.

Maheady, L., Mallette, B., Harper, G. F., & Sacca, K. (1991). Heads together: A peer-mediated option for improving the academic achievement of heterogeneous learning groups. Remedial and Special Education, 12(2), 25-33.

Maheady, L., Sacca, M. K., & Harper, G. F. (1987). Classwide student tutoring teams: Effects on the academic performance of secondary students. Journal of Special Education, 12(2), 107-121.

Manset, G., & Semmel, M. I. (1997). Are inclusive programs for students with mild disabilities effective? A comparative review of model programs. Journal of Special Education, 31(2), 155- 180.

Martin, E. W. Case studies on inclusion: Worst rears realized. The Journal of Special Education, 29(2), 192-199.

Mathur, S. R., & Rutherford, R. B. (1991). Peer-mediated interventions promoting social skills of children and youth with behavioral disorders. Education and Treatment of Children, 14(3), 227- 242.

Mavis V. Sobel, 20 IDELR 1125 (N.D.N.Y. 1994).

McCarthy, B. (1980). The 4MAT system: Teaching to learning styles with right/left mode techniques. Barrington, IL: EXCEL, Inc.

McDonnell, J. (1987). The integration of students with severe handicaps into regular public schools: An analysis of parents perceptions of potential outcomes. Education and Training in Mental Retardation, 22(2), 98-111.

McDonnell, J., Hardman, M., Hightower, J., & Kiefer-O'Donnell, R. (1991). Variables associated with in-school and after-school integration of secondary students with severe disabilities. Education and Training in Mental Retardation, 26, 243-257.

McDonnell, J., Thorson, N., McQuivey, C., & Kiefer-O'Donnell, R. (1997). Academic engaged time of students with low-incidence disabilities in general education classes. Mental Retardation, 35(1), 18-26.

McDougall, D., & Brady, M. P. (1998). Initiating and fading self-management interventions to increase math fluency in general education classes. Exceptional Children, 64(2), 151-166.

McIntosh, R., Vaughn, S., Schumm, J. S., Haager, D., & Lee, O. (1994). Observations of students with learning disabilities in general education classrooms. Exceptional Children, 60(3), 249-261.

McLaughlin, M. W. (1990, December). The Rand change agent study revisited: Macro perspectives and micro realities. Educational Researcher, 19, 11-16.

McLaughlin, M. W., & Warren, S. H. (1994, November). The costs of inclusion: Reallocating financial and human resources to include students with disabilities. The School Administrator, 51, 8-18.

McNulty, B. A., Rogers Connolly, T., Wilson, P. G., & Brewer, R. D. (1996). LRE policy. The leadership challenge. Remedial and Special Education, 17(3), 158-167.

Merrow, J. (1996, May 8). What's so special about special education? Education Week, 15(33), 48, 38.

Meyer, L.. H., Minondo, S., Fisher, M., Larson, M. J., Dunmore, S., Black, J. W., & D'Aquanni, M. (1998). Frames of friendships. Social relationships among adolescents with diverse abilities. In L. H. Meyer, H Park, M. Grenot-Scheyer, I. S. Schwartz & B. Harry (Eds.), Making friends: The influences of culture and development (pp. 189-218). Baltimore: Paul H. Brookes.

Meyers, J., Gelzheiser, L. M., & Yelich, G. (1991). Do pull-in programs foster teacher collaboration? Remedial and Special Education, 12(2), 7-15.

Miles, M. B., & Huberman, A. M. (1984). Innovation up close: How school improvement works. New York: Plenum Press.

Miller, L. J., Strain, P. S., Boyd, K., Hunsicker, S., McKinley, J., & Wu, A. (1992). Parent attitudes toward integration. Topics in Early Childhood Special Education, 12, 230-246.

Miller, R. A. What's up in factories? Educational Leadership, 53(8), 30-32.

Miller, T. L., & Sabatino, D. (1978). An evaluation of the teacher consultation model as an approach to mainstreaming. Exceptional Children, 45(2), 86-91.

Minke, K. M., Bear, G. G., Deemer, S. A., & Griffin, S. M. (1996). Teachers' experiences with inclusive classrooms: Implications for special education reform. Journal of Special Education, 30(2), 152-186.

Mok, P. P. (1975). Communicating styles survey. Dallas, TX: Training Associates Press.

Monda-Amaya, L. E., & Pearson, P. D. (1996). Toward a responsible pedagogy for teaching and learning literacy. In M. C. Pugach & C. L. Warger (Eds.), Curriculum trends, special education, and reform. Refocusing the conversation (pp. 143-163). New York: Teachers College Press.

Myers, I. B. (1962). Introduction to type. Palo Alto, CA: Consulting Psychologists Press. Inc.

Myers, I. B., & Briggs, K. C. (1976). Myers-Briggs type indicator. Palo Alto, CA: Consulting Psychologists Press, Inc.

National Center of Educational Restructuring and Inclusion (1994). National study of inclusive education. New York: City University of New York, NCERI.

National Center on Educational Restructuring and Inclusion (1995). National study of inclusive education. New York: City University of New York, NCERI.

National Commission on Excellence in Education (1983). A nation at risk: The imperative for educational reform. Washington, DC: U.S. Government Printing Office.

National Educational Association (1994). Time strategies. Author.

Nelson, C. M., & Stevens, K. B. (1981). An accountable consultation model for mainstreaming behaviorarlly disordered children. Behavioral Disorders, 6(2), 82-91.

Nevin, A., Paolucci-Whitcomb, P., Dancan, D., & Thibodeau, . A. (1982). The consulting teacher as clinical researcher. Teacher Education and Special Education, 5, 19-29.

Newmann, F., & Wehlage, G. G. (1993). Five standards of authentic instruction. Educational Leadership, 50(7), 8-12.

Newmann, F., & Wehlage, G. (1995). Successful school restructuring. Alexandria, VA: Association of Supervision and Curriculum Development.

Newton, J. S., & Horner, R. H. (1993). Using a social guide to improve social relationships of people with severe disabilities. Journal of the Association for Persons with Severe Handicaps, 18(1), 36- 45.

Nicholls, J. G. (1989). The competitive ethos and democratic education. Boston: Harvard University Press.

Oakes, J., & Lipton, M. (1992). Detracking schools: Early lessons from the field. Phi Delta Kappan, 448-454.

Oakes, J., & Wells, A. (1996). Beyond the technicalities of school reform. Policy lessons from detracking schools. Los Angeles, CA: UCLA Graduate School of Education and Information Studies.

Oakes, J., Wells, A. S., Yonezawa, S., & Ray, K. (1997). Equity lessons from detracking schools. In A. Hargreaves (Ed.), 1997 ASCD yearbook. Rethinking educational change with heart and mind. Alexandria, VA: Association for Supervision and Curriculum Development.

Oberti v. Board of Education, 995 F.2d 1204 (3rd. Cir. 1993).

O'Connor, R. E., & Jenkins, J. R. (1996). Cooperative learning as an inclusion strategy: A closer look. Exceptionality, 6(1), 29-51.

Odom, S. L., Deklyen, M., & Jenkins, J. R. (1984). Integrating handicapped and nonhandicapped preschoolers: Developmental impact on nonhandicapped children. Exceptional Children, 51(1), 41- 48.

Odom, S., & Strain, P. S. (1986). A comparison of peer-initiation and teacher-antecedent interventions for promoting reciprocal social interaction of autistic preschoolers. Journal of Applied Behavior Analysis, 19, 59-71.

Olson, M. R., Chalmers, L., & Hoover, J. H. (1997). Attitudes and attributes of general education teachers identified as effective inclusionists. Remedial and Special Education, 18(1), 28-35.

O'Neil, J. (1995). Can inclusion work? A conversation with Jim Kauffman and Mara Sapon-Shevin. Educational Leadership, 52(4), 7-11.

Osguthorpe, R. T. & Scruggs, T. E. (1986). Special education students as tutors: A review and analysis. Remedial and Special Education, 7, 15-26.

Paley, V. 1992). You can't say you can't play. Cambridge, MA: Harvard University Press.

Palmer, D. S., Borthwick-Duggy, S. A., & Widaman, K. (1998). Parent perceptions of inclusive practices for their children with significant cognitive disabilities. Exceptional Children, 64(1), 271- 282.

Pavan, B. N. (1973). Good news: Research on the nongraded elementary school. Elementary School Journal, 73, 233-242.

Pearman, E. L., Barnhart, M., Huang, A., & Melblom, C. (1992). Educating all students in general education: Attitudes and beliefs about inclusion. Educational and Training in Mental Retardation, 27, 176-182.

Pearman, E., Huang, A. M., & Mellblom, C. I. (1997). The inclusion of all students: Concerns and incentives of educators. Educational and Training in Mental Retardation and Developmental Disabilities, 32(1), 11-20.

Peck, C. A., Carlson, P., & Helmstetter, E. (1992). Parent and teacher perceptions of outcomes for typically developing children enrolled in integrated early childhood programs: A statewide survey. Journal of Early Intervention, 16, 53-63.

Peck, C. A., Donaldson, J., & Pezzoli, M. (1990). Some benefits adolescents perceive for themselves from their social relationships with peers who have severe disabilities. Journal of the Association for Persons with Severe Handicaps, 15(4), 241-249.

Peck, C. A., Killen, C., & Baumgart, D. (1989). Increasing implementation of special education instruction in mainstream preschools: Direct and generalized effects of nondirective consultation. Journal of Applied Behavior Analysis, 22(2), 197-210.

Perkins, D., & Blythe, T. (1994). Putting understanding up front. Educational Leadership, 51(5), 4-7.

Polakow, V. (1992). Invisible voices and visible spaces: Do young children matter existentially? The Review of Education, 14(4), 295-203.

Pool, H., & Page, J. A. (1995). Beyond tracking. Finding success in inclusive schools. Bloomington, IN: Phi Delta Kappa Educational Foundation.

Poolaw v. Parker Unified School District, 21 IDELR 1 (D. Ariz. 1994).

Porro, B. (1996). Talk it out. Conflict resolution in the elementary classroom. Alexandria, VA: ASCD.

Prescott, C., Rinard, B., Cocerill, J., & Baker, N. (1996). Science through workplace lenses. Educational Leadership, 53(8), 11-13.

Pugach, M. (1995). On the failure of imagination in inclusive schooling. The Journal of Special Education, 29(2), 212-223.

Pugach, M. C., & Johnson, L. J. (1995). Unlocking expertise among classroom teachers through structured dialogue: Extending research on peer collaboration. Exceptional Children, 62(2), 101- 110.

Pugach, M. C., & Warger, C. L. (1996a). Treating curriculum as a target of reform: can special and general education learn from each other? In M. C. Pugach & C. L. Warger (Eds.), Curriculum trends, special education, and reform. Refocusing the conversation (pp. 1-22). New York: Teachers College Press.

Pugach, M. C., & Warger, C. L. (1996b). Challenges for the special education-curriculum reform partnership. In M. C. Pugach & C. L. Warger (Eds.), Curriculum trends, special education, and reform. Refocusing the conversation (pp. 227-252). New York: Teachers College Press.

Pugach, M. C., & Wesson, C. (1995). Teachers' and students' views of team teaching of general education and learning-disabled students in two fifth-grade classes. The Elementary School Journal, 95, 279-295.

Putnam, J. W., Rynders, J. E., Johnson, R. T., & Johnson, D. W. (1989). Collaborative skill instruction for promoting positive interactions between mentally handicapped and nonhandicapped children. Exceptional Children, 55, 550-558.

Raywid, M. A. (1993). Finding time for collaboration. Educational Leadership, 51(1), 30-34.

Reichart, D. C., Lynch, E. C., Anderson, B. C., Svobodny, L. A., DiCola, J. M., & Mercury, M. G. (1989). Parental perspectives on integrated preschool opportunities for children with handicaps and children without handicaps. Journal of Early Intervention, 13(1), 6-13.

Reissman, R. (1995). In search of ordinary heroes. Educational Leadership, 52(8), 28-31.

Roach, V. (1995). Winning ways: Creating inclusive schools, classrooms and communities. Alexandria, VA: National Association of State Boards of Education.

Rosenfield, S. (1987). Instructional consultation. Hillsdale, NJ: Lawrence Erlbaum Associates.

Rosjewski, J. W., & Pollard, R. R. (1990). A multivariate analysis of perceptions held by secondary academic teachers toward students with special needs. Teacher Education and Special Education, 13, 149-153.

Rudduck, J. (1991). Innovation and change: Developing involvement and understanding. Buckingham: Open University Press.

Ryan, K. (1993). Mining the values in the curriculum. Educational Leadership, 54(1), 16-18.

Ryndak, D. L., Downing, J. E., Morrison, A. P., & Williams, L. J. (1996). Parents' perceptions of educational settings and services for children with moderate or severe disabilities. Remedial and Special Education, 17(2), 106-118.

Sacramento City Unified School District v. Rachel H., 14 F.3d 1398 (9th Cir. 1994).

Sage, D. D., & Burrello, L. C. (1994). Leadership in educational reform. Baltimore: Paul H. Brookes.

Sale, P., & Carey, D. M. (1995). The sociometric status of students with disabilities in a full-inclusion school. Exceptional Children, 62, 6-19.

Salend, S. J., Johansen, M., Mumper, J., Chase, A. S., Pike, K. M., & Dorney, J. A. (1997). Cooperative teaching. The voices of two teachers. Remedial and Special Education, 18(1), 3-11.

Salisbury, C., & Chambers, A. (1994). Instructional costs of inclusive schooling. Journal of the Association for Persons with Severe Handicaps, 19(3), 215-222.

Salisbury, C. L., Evans, I. M., & Palombaro, M. M. (1997). Collaborative problem-solving to promote the inclusion of young children with significant disabilities in primary grades. Exceptional Children, 63(2), 195-210.

Salisbury, C. L., Gallucci, C., Palombaro, M. M., & Peck, C. A. (1995). Strategies that promote social relations among elementary students with and without severe disabilities in inclusive schools. Exceptional Children, 62(2), 125-137.

Salisbury, C. L., & Palombaro, M. M. (1998). Friends and acquaintances: Evolving relationships in an inclusive elementary school. In L. H. Meyer, H. Park, M. Grenot-Scheyer, I. S. Schwartz & B. Harry (Eds.), Making friends. The influences of culture and development (pp. 81-104). Baltimore: Paul H. Brookes.

Salisbury, C. L., Palombaro, M. M.,& Hollowood, T. M. (1993). On the nature and change of an inclusive elementary school. Journal of the Association for Persons with Severe Handicaps, 18(2), 75-84.

Salisbury, C. L., Wilson, L., Swartz, T., Palombaro, M., & Wassel, J. (1997). Using action research to solve instructional challenges in inclusive elementary school settings. Education and Treatment of Children, 20(1), 21-39.

Sapon-Shevin, M. (1994/1995). Why gifted students belong in inclusive schools. Educational Leadership, 54(4), 64-70.

Sapon-Shevin, M., Dobbelaere, A., Corrigan, C. R., Goodman, K., & Mastin, M. C. (1998). Promoting inclusive behavior in inclusive classrooms. "You can't say you can't play". In L. H. Meyer, H. Park, M. Grenot-Scheyer, I. S. Schwartz & B. Harry (Eds.), Making friends. The influences of culture and development (pp. 105-132). Baltimore: Paul H. Brookes.

Sarason, S. (1990). The predictable failure of educational reform. San Francisco: Jossey-Bass.

Sasso, G. M., Hughes, G. G., Swanson, H. L., & Novak, C. G. (1987). A comparison of peer initiation interventions in promoting multiple peer initiators. Education and Training in Mental Retardation, 22, 150-155.

Sasso, G. M., & Rude, H. A. (1987). Unprogrammed effects of training high-status peers to interact with severely handicapped children. Journal of Applied Behavior Analysis, 20, 35-44.

Schafer, W., & Olexa, C. (1971). Tracking and opportunity: The locking-out process and beyond. Scranton, PA: Chandler.

Schaffner, C. B., & Buswell, B. E. (1996). Ten critical elements for creating inclusive and effective school communities. In S. Stainback & W. Stainback (Eds.), Inclusion. A guide for educators (pp. 49-65). Baltimore: Paul H. Brookes.

Schaps, E. (1997, January 22). Pushing back for the center. Education Week, 16(17), 20.

Schattman, R. (1992). The Franklin Northwest Supervisory Union. In R. Villa, J. Thousand, W. Stainback, & S. Stainback (Eds.), Restructuring for caring and effective education: An administrative guide to creating heterogeneous schools (pp. 143-159). Baltimore: Paul H. Brookes.

Schlechty, P. (1990). Schools for the 21st century: Leadership imperatives for educational reform. San Francisco: Jossey-Bass.

Schnaiberg, L. (1996). Educating Rafael: When a child has Down syndrome, who decides what kind of education is "best"? Education Week, 15(16), 18-26.

Schneider, E. (1996). Giving students a voice in the classroom. Educational Leadership, 54(1), 22-26.

Schnorr, R. F. (1990). "Peter? He comes and goes.....". First graders' perspectives on a part-time mainstream student. Journal of the Association for Persons with Severe Handicaps, 15(4), 231- 240.

Schnorr, R. F. (1997). From enrollment to membership: "Belonging" in middle and high school classes. Journal of the Association for Persons with Severe Handicaps, 22(1), 1-15.

Schulz, J. B., Carpenter, C. D., & Turnbull, A. P. (1991). Mainstreaming exceptional students. A guide for classroom teachers (Third edition). Boston: Allyn & Bacon.

Schulte, A., Osborne, S., & McKinney, J. (1990). Academic outcomes for students with learning disability in consultation and resource programs. Exceptional Children, 57(2), 162-171.

Schumaker, J. B., Deshler, D. D., Alley, G. R., & Warner, M. M. (1983). Toward the development of an intervention model for learning disabled adolescents. Exceptional Education Quarterly, 3(4), 45- 50.

Schumaker, J. B., Deshler, D. D., & Ellis, E. S. (1986). Intervention issues related to the education of LD adolescents. In J. K. Torgeson & B. Y. L. Wong (Eds.), Learning disabilities: Some new perspectives. New York: Academic Press.

Schumnn, J. S., & Vaughn, S. (1991). Making adaptations for mainstreamed students. Remedial and Special Education, 12(4), 18-27.

Schumm, J. S., & Vaughn, S. (1992). Planning for mainstreamed special education students: Perceptions of general classroom teachers. Exceptionality, 3, 81-98.

Schumm, J. S., Vaughn, S., Gordon, J., & Rothlein, L. (1994). General education teachers' beliefs, skills, and practices in planning for mainstreamed students with learning disabilities. Teacher Education and Special Education, 17, 22-37.

Schumm, J. S., Vaughn, S., Haager, D., McDowell, J., Rothlein, L., & Saumell, L. (1995). General education teacher planning: What can students with learning disabilities expect? Exceptional Children, 61(4), 335-352.

Scruggs, T. E., & Mastropieri, M. A. (1996). Teacher perceptions of mainstreaming/inclusion, 1958-1995: A research synthesis. Exceptional Children, 63(1), 59-74.

Scruggs, T. E., & Osguthorpe, R. T. (1986). Tutoring interventions within special education settings: A comparison of cross-age and peer tutoring. Psychology in the Schools, 23, 187-193.

Semmel, M., Abernathy, T., Butera, G., & Lesar, S. (1991). Teacher perceptions of the regular education initiative. Exceptional Children, 57, 9-22.

Sergiovanni, T. J. (1994). Building community in schools. San Francisco: Jossey-Bass.

Sharan, S. (1980). Cooperative learning in small groups: Recent methods and effects on achievement, attitudes and ethnic relations. Review of Educational Research, 50, 241-271.

Sharan, S., & Hertz-Lazarowitz, R. (1980). A group investigation method of cooperative learning in the classroom. In S. Sharan, P. Hard, C. Webb & R. Hertz-Lazarowitz (Eds.), Cooperation in education (pp. 14-46). Provo, UT: Brigham Young University Press.

Sharan, Y., & Sharan, S. (1992). Expanding cooperative learning through group investigation. New York: Teachers College Press.

Sharpe, M. N., York, J. L., & Knight, J. (1994). Effects of inclusion on the academic performance of classmates without disabilities. Remedial and Special Education, 15(5), 281-287.

Simpson, R. L., & Myles, B. S. (1989). Parents' mainstreaming modification preferences for children with educable mental handicaps, behavior disorders, and learning disabilities. Psychology in the Schools, 26, 292-301.

Sinson, J. C., & Wetherick, N. E. (1981). The behavior of children with Down's Syndrome in normal playgroups. Journal of Mental Deficiency Research, 25, 113-120.

Slavin, R. E. (1987). Ability grouping and student achievement in elementary schools: A best-evidence synthesis. Review of Educational Research, 57(3), 293-336.

Slavin, R. E. (1990a). Ability grouping, cooperative learning, and the gifted. Journal for the Education of the Gifted, 14(1), 3-8.

Slavin, R. E. (1990b). Achievement effects of ability grouping in secondary schools: A best-evidence synthesis. Review of Educational Research, 60(3), 471-499.

Slavin, R. E. (1990c). Cooperative learning. Theory, research, and practice. Englewood Cliffs, NJ: Prentice Hall.

Slavin, R. E. (1990d). Ability grouping and student achievement in secondary schools. Review of Educational Research, 60, 417-499.

Slavin, R., Schlomo, S., Spencer, K., Webb, C., & Schmuck, R. (1985). Learning to cooperate, cooperating to learn. New York: Plenum Press.

Smelter, R. W., Rasch, B. W., & Yudewitz, G. J. (1994). Thinking of inclusion for all special needs students? Better think again. Phi Delta Kappan, 76(1), 35-38.

Snyder, L., Apolloni, T., & Cooke, T. P. (1977). Integrated settings at the early childhood level: The role of nonretarded peers. Exceptional Children, 43, 262-266.

Solomon, D., Schaps, E., Watson, M., & Battistich, V. (1992). Creating caring school and classroom communities for all students. In R. A. Villa, J. S. Thousand, W. .Stainback & S. Stainback (Eds.), Restructuring for caring and effective education (pp. 41-60). Baltimore: Paul H. Brookes.

Speece, D., & Mandell, C. (1980). Resource room support services for regular classroom teachers. Learning Disabilities Quarterly, 3, 49-53.

Stainback, W., & Stainback, S. (1990). Support networks for inclusive schooling: Interdependent integrated education. Baltimore: Paul H. Brookes.

Stainback, W., Stainback, S., Moravec, J., & Jackson, H. J. (1992). Concerns about full inclusion: An ethnographic investigation. In R. Villa, J. Thousand, W. Stainback, & S. Stainback (Eds.), Restructuring for caring and effective education: An administrative guide to creating heterogeneous schools (pp. 305-324). Baltimore: Paul H. Brookes.

Stainback, W., Stainback, S., Stefanich, G., & Alper, S. (1996). Learning in inclusive classrooms. What about the curriculum? In S. Stainback & W. Stainback (Eds.), Inclusion. A guide for educators (pp. 209-219). Baltimore: Paul H. Brookes.

Staub, D., & Hunt, P. (1993). The effects of social interaction training on high school peer tutors of schoolmates with severe disabilities. Exceptional Children, 60(1), 41-57.

Staub, D., Schwartz, I. L., Gallucci, C., & Peck, C. A. (1994). Four portraits of friendship at an inclusive school. Journal of the Association for Persons with Severe Handicaps, 19(4), 314-325.

Staub, D., Spaulding, M., Peck, C. A., Gallucci, C., & Schwartz, I. S. (1996). Using nondisabled peers to support the inclusion of students with disabilities at the junior high school level. Journal of the Association of Persons with Severe Handicaps, 21(4), 194-205.

Stepien, W., & Gallagher, S. (1993). Problem-based leraning: As authentic as it gets. Educational Leadership, 50(7), 25-28.

Sternberg, . R. J. (1994) Diversifying instruction and assessment. The Educational Forum, 59(1), 47- 53.

Sternberg, R. J. (1997). What does it mean to be smart? Educational Leadership, 54(6), 20-24.

Sternberg, R. J., & Spear-Swerling, L. (1996). Teaching for thinking. Washington, DC: American Psychological Association.

Stoll, L., & Fink, D. (1996). Changing our schools. Buckingham and Philadelphia: Open University Press.

Strain, P. S., & Odom, S. L. (1986). A comparison of peer-initiation and teacher-antecedent interventions for promoting reciprocal social interaction of autistic preschoolers. Journal of Applied Behavior Analysis, 19, 59-71.

Strain, P. S., Shores, R. E., & Timm, M. A. (1977). Effects of peer social initiations on the behavior of withdrawn preschool children: Some training and generalization effects. Journal of Applied Behavior Analysis, 10, 289-298.

Teele, S. (1995). The multiple intelligences school. A place for all students to succeed. Redlands, CA: Citrograph Printing.

Thompson, S. (1995). The community as classroom. Educational Leadership, 52(8), 17-20.

Thousand, J. S., & Villa, R. A. (1990). Sharing expertise and responsibilities through teaching teams. In W. Stainback & S. Stainback (Eds.), Support networks for inclusive schooling (pp. 151-166). Baltimore: Paul H. Brookes.

Thousand, J. S., & Villa, R. A. (1995). Managing complex change toward inclusive schooling. In R. A. Villa & J. S. Thousand (Eds.), Creating an inclusive school (pp. 51-79). Alexandria, VA: Association for Supervision and Curriculum Development.

Tralli, R., Colombo, B., Deshler, D. D., & Schumaker, J. B. (1996). The strategies intervention model: A model for supported inclusion at the secondary level. Remedial and Special Education, 17(4), 204-216.

Turiel, E. (1987). Potential relations between the development of social reasoning and childhood aggression. In D. Crowell, I. M. Evans, & C. R. O'Donnell (Eds.), Childhood aggression and violence: Sources of influence, prevention and control (pp. 124-135). New York: Plenum Press.

Turnbull, A., & Schultz, J. B. (1979). Mainstreaming handicapped students. Boston: Allyn & Bacon.

Turnbull, A. P., & Winton, P. (1983). A comparison of specialized and mainstreamed preschools from the perspectives of parents of handicapped children. Journal of Pediatric Psychology, 8(1), 57-71.

Turnbull, A. P., Winton, P. J., Blacher, J., & Salkind, N. (1982). Mainstreaming in the kindergarten classroom: Perspectives of parents of handicapped and nonhandicapped children. Journal of the Division for Early Childhood, 6, 14-20.

Tymitz-Wolf, B. (1984). An analysis of EMR children's worries about mainstreaming. Educational and Training in Mental Retardation, 19, 157-167.

Udvari-Solner, A. (1995). A process for adapting curriculum in inclusive classrooms. In R. A. Villa & J. Thousand (Eds.), Creating an inclusive school (pp. 110-124). Alexandria, VA: Association of Supervision and Curriculum Development.

Udvari-Solner, A., & Thousand, J. (1995). Exemplary and promising teaching practices that foster inclusive education. In R. Villa & J. Thousand (Eds.), Creating an inclusive school (pp. 87-109). Alexandria, VA: Association of Supervision and Curriculum Development.

Udvari-Solner, A., & Thousand, J. S. (1996). Creating a responsive curriculum for inclusive schools. Remedial and Special Education, 17(3), 182-192.

U.S. Department of Education (1996). To assure the free appropriate public education of all children with disabilities. Eighteenth annual report to Congress on the implementation of IDEA. Washington, DC: author.

Vaughn, S., & Schumm, J. S. (1994). Middle school teachers' planning for students with disabilities. Remedial and Special Education, 15, 152-161.

Vickery, T. R. (1987). Excellence in an outcome-driven school district: A validation study of the schools of Johnson City, New York. Syracuse, NY: Syracuse University.

Villa, R. A., Thousand, J. S., Meyers, H., & Nevin, A. (1996). Teacher and administrator perceptions of heterogeneous education. Exceptional Children, 63(1), 29-45.

Villa, R. A., Thousand, J. S., Nevin, A. I., & Malgeri, C. (1996). Instilling collaboration for inclusive schooling as a way of doing business in public schools. Remedial and Special Education, 17(3), 169-181.

Voeltz, L. M. (1980). Children's attitudes toward handicapped peers. American Journal of Mental Deficiency, 84(5), 455-464.

Voeltz, L. M. (1982). Effects of structured interactions with severely handicapped peers on children's attitudes. American Journal of Mental Deficiency, 86(4), 380-390.

Wacker, D. P., & Berg, W. K. (1985). Use of peers to train and monitor the performance of adolescents with severe handicaps. Education and Training of the Mentally Retarded, 20(2), 109-122.

Wagner, P., & Sternlicht, M. (1975). Retarded persons as "teachers": Retarded adolescents tutoring retarded children. American Journal of Mental Deficiency, 79, 674-679.

Walter-Thomas, C. S. (1997) Co-teaching experiences: The benefits and problems that teachers and principals report over time. Journal of Learning Disabilities, 30(4), 395-407.

Walter-Thomas, C., Bryant, M., & Land, S. (1996). Planning for effective co-teaching. Remedial and Special Education, 17(4), 255-cover 3.

Wang, M. C., & Birch, J. W. (1984). Comparison of a full-time mainstreaming program and a resource room approach. Exceptional Children, 51(1), 33-40.

Wehman. P., Kregel, J., & Seyfarth, J. (1985). Transition from school to work for individuals with severe handicaps: A follow-up study. Journal of the Association for Persons with Severe Handicaps, 10(3), 132-136.

Werts, M. G., Wolery, M., Snyder, E. D., Caldwell, N. K., & Salisbury, C. L. (1996). Supports and resources associated with inclusive schooling: Perceptions of elementary school teachers about need and availability. Journal of Special Education, 30(2), 187-203.

West, J. F., & Idol, L. (1987). School consultation (Part I): An interdisciplinary perspective on theory, models, and research. Journal of Learning Disabilities, 20, 388-408.

Wheelock, A. (1992). Crossing the tracks. How "untracking" can save America's schools. New York: New Press.

Whinnery, K. W., Fuchs, L. S., & Fuchs, D. (1991). General, special, and remedial teachers' acceptance of behavioral and instructional strategies for mainstreaming. Remedial and Special Education, 12(4), 6-17.

Whitaker & Moses (1994). The restructuring handbook. A guide to school revitalization. Boston: Allyn & Bacon.

Williams, D. (1990). Listening to today's teachers: They can tell us what tomorrow's teachers should know. Teacher Education and Special Education, 13, 149-153.

Witkin, H. A., Moore, C. A., Goodenough, D. R., & Cox, P. W. (1977). Field-dependent and field-independent cognitive styles and their educational implications. Review of Educational Research, 47(1), 1-64.

Wolery, M., Anthony, L., Snyder, E. D., Werts, M. G., & Katzenmeyer, J. (1997). Effective instructional practices in inclusive classrooms. Education and Treatment of Children, 20(1), 50-58.

Wolery, M., Werts, M. G., Caldwell, N. K., Snyder, E. D., & Liskowski, L. (1995). Experienced teachers' perceptions of resources and supports for inclusion. Educational and Training in Mental Retardation and Developmental Disabilities, 30(1), 1-26.

Wood, M. (1998). Whose job is it anyway? Educational roles in inclusion. Exceptional Children, 64(1), 181-196.

Wright, S., & Cowen, E. L. (1985). Effects of peer teaching on student perceptions of class environments, adjustment, and academic performance. American Journal of Community Psychology, 13, 417-431.

York, J., Vandercook, T., MacDonald, C., Heise-Neff, C., & Caughey, E. (1992). Feedback about integrating middle-school students with severe disabilities in general education classes. Exceptional Children, 58, 244-258.

York, J., & Tundidor, H. (1995). Issues raised in the name of inclusion: Perspectives of educators, parents, and students. Journal of the Association for Persons with Severe Handicaps, 20, 31-44.

York-Barr, J. (1996). Introduction to the topical issue. Remedial and Special Education, 17(3), 131- 133.

York-Barr, J., Kronberg, R. M., & Doyle, M. B. (1996). Creating inclusive school communities. Module 4 - Collaboration: Redefining roles, practices, and structures. Baltimore: Paul H. Brookes.

York-Barr, J., Schultz, T., Doyle, M. B., Kronberg, R., & Crossett, S. (1996). Inclusive schooling in St. Cloud. Remedial and Special Education, 17(2), 92-105.

Zahn, G. L., Kagan, S., & Widaman, K. F. (1986). Cooperative learning and classroom climate. Journal of School Psychology, 24, 351-362.

Zemelman, S., Daniels, H., & Hyde, A. (1993). Best practice. New standards for teaching and learning in America's schools. Portsmouth, NH: Heinemann.

Zigmond, N. (1995). An exploration of the meaning and practice of special educationin the context of full inclusion of students with learning disabilities. The Journal of Special Education, 29(2), 109- 115.

Zigmond, N. (1995a). Inclusion in Pennsylvania: Educational experiences of students with learning disabilities in one elementary school. The Journal of Special Education, 29(2), 124-132.

Zigmond, N. (1995b). Inclusion in Kansas: Educational experiences of students with learning disabilities in one elementary school. The Journal of Special Education, 29(2), 144-154.

Zigmond, N., & Baker, J. M. (1990). Mainstreaming experiences for learning disabled students (Project MELD): Preliminary report. Exceptional Children, 57, 176-185.

Zigmond, N., & Baker, J. M. (1995). Concluding comments: Current and future practices in inclusive schooling. Journal of Special Education, 29(2), 245-250.

Appendix A:

Summary of District and Federal Court Decision About Inclusion

Summary of District and Federal Court Decisions About Inclusion[1]

Decisions Supporting Inclusive Placements	Decisions Against Inclusive Placements
Daniel R. R. v. State Board of Education (1989): Ruling in favor of regular class placement for a child with mental retardation, the court established a standard for determining when placement in a regular education class is appropriate, and when removal is educationally justified.	Clyde K. and Sheila K. v. Puyallup School District (1995): Ruling in favor of the school district, the court supported their decision to remove a students with Tourettes syndrome from general education classes, placing him in a separate program due to his disruptive behavior in the general education classroom.
Greer v. Rome City School District (1991): Ruling in favor of regular class placement for a student with Down syndrome, the court found that the district failed to consider the full ranse of supplemental aids and services that could assist the child in the regular education classroom, and failed to modify the curriculum to accommodate the student's needs.	Poolaw v. Parker Unified School District (1994): Ruling in favor of the school district, an Arizona district court did not support the wishes of the parents of 13 year olf Native American student who is deaf to attend his local school. Instead, the student was ordered to be placed in the state's School for the Deaf because the student's language skills were so poor.
Oberti v. Board of Education (1993): Ruling in favor of regular class placement for a student with Down syndrome, the court found that the district effort's to accommodate the students in the regular class were insufficient. Emphasis was placed on the use of supplementary aids and services as a means of accommodating the student.	Kari H. V. Franklin S.S.D.(1995): Ruling in favor of the school district, a federal judge in Tennessee ordered a 14 year old student requiring extensive supports to be placed in a separate special education class with some mainstreaming, in spite of a history of regular class placement in another state. The school district argued that their attempts to provide a regular class did not benefit the student, and was disruptive to other students.
Sacramento City Unified School District v. Rachel Holland (1994): Ruling in favor of regular class placement for a student with Down Syndrome, the court affirmed and adoped the analysis and standards outlined in the previous federal court decisions.	Hudson v. Bloomfield Hills School District (1995): Ruling in favor of the school district, a federal district court in Michigan upheld the placement of a 14 year old student with mental retardation in a separate classroom. The district testified that the student had not benefitted during his time in a placement that split his time between general and special education in two different schools.

Decisions Supporting Inclusive Placements

Mavis v. Sobol (1994): Ruling in favor of the family, the court found the district's plan to place a student with mental retardation in a special education classroom with mainstreaming for nonacademic subjects only violated the LRE standard.

Norma P. et al. v. Pelham School District (1995): Ruling in favor of a New Hampshire school district, the court rejected the wishes of the family of a teenager with Down syndrome who opposed an inclusive placement.

Decisions Against Inclusive Placements

D.F. v. Western School Corp (1996): Ruling in favor of the school district, a 13 year old student with multiple disability was ordered by an Indiana federal district court judge to be placed in a special education classroom. He found that the curricular modifications necessary to accommodate this student in the general education classroom were too extensive.

Evans v. Board of Education (1996): Ruling in favor of the parents of a 15 year old boy with dyslexia, a federal district court judge ordered that an IEP be developed that enabled this student to attend classes with students who have similar disabilities.

Fort Zumwalt School District v. Board of Education (1996): Ruling in favor of the parents of a third-grade student with learning disabilities, a federal district court judge found that the school district should not have placed him in the general education classroom. The rationale for the decision was that the child's self-esteem and behavior problems were aggravated by being around students that made him feel "different".

¹Information summarized from Lipton (1994) and Lipsky & Gartner (1997), Chapter 9.

Appendix B:

Research Study Tables

Table B-1
Documented Outcomes for Students with Disabilities in Inclusive Settings

Study	Design	Setting	Sample[1]	Duration[2]	Intervention/ Analysis	Data Sources	Findings
Affleck, Madge, Adams, & Lowen-braun, 1988	nonequiva-lent control group design	integrated classes and resource rooms	137 students with LD; 39 general ed students	3 years	Comparison of student performance across settings; examine cost-effectiveness	Reading, math, language subtests of Woodcock Johnson; California Achievement Test; district cost data	◆ No differences in performance of students with LD in resource or integrated classrooms ◆ No differences in performance of typical children in integrated vs. non-integrated classrooms ◆ Integrated model found to be more cost effective while achieving similar results
Brady, Shores, McEvoy, Ellis & Fox, 1987	multiple baseline design	elementary school	1 swsd; 8 typical peers	47 days	Student taught to initiate interaction with typical peers	Direct observation	◆ Level of initiation and interaction increased with trained and untrained peers after two typical peers were involved ◆ Result continued to improve as third student was involved in intervention
Brinker, 1985	group comparison design	14 school districts in 9 states	245 swsd, aged 3-22	1 school year	Comparison of rate of social interaction in groups with and without typical peers	Direct observation	◆ Greater opportunities for social interaction in integrated groups ◆ Typical students interacted with students w/sd more frequently than peers with disabilities

Study	Design	Setting	Sample[1]	Duration[2]	Intervention/ Analysis	Data Sources	Findings
Brinker & Thorpe, 1984	predictive study - multiple linear regression	14 school districts in 9 states	245 swsd, aged 3-22	1 school year	Examine learning rates relative to degree of integration with typical peers	Student IEPs; direct observation; measure of adaptive behavior	◆ Degree of integration was a significant predictor of educational progress as measured by proportion of IEP objectives met
Brinker & Thorpe, 1986	predictive study - regression & commonality analysis	14 school districts in 9 states	245 swsd aged 3-22	1 school year	Examine features of learning environments that predict social behavior	Direct observation; measure of adaptive behavior; IEPs; school & teacher support for integration	◆ Variance in degree of integration associated with social behavior directed to student w/sd by typical peers ◆ Data suggests integration can be best fostered by teaching typical students strategies for maintaining interactive behavior with peers w/sd
Cole & Meyer, 1991	group comparison study	5 students were in separate settings; 36 attended regular schools	91 swsd	2 years	Comparison of social competence of students w/sd in segregated vs inclusive settings	Classroom observation; Assessment of Social Competence; TARC	◆ Children in inclusive settings spent less time with therapists, equal time with sped teachers, more time with assistants, more time with peers, and less time alone than those in segregated settings ◆ Children in inclusive settings demonstrated greater progress on measure of social competence

Study	Design	Setting	Sample[1]	Duration[2]	Intervention/ Analysis	Data Sources	Findings
Eichinger, 1990	series of ABAB designs	2 elementary schools	8 typical students	8 swsd 6 weeks	Comparison of social interaction rates based on task structures	Direct observation	◆ Cooperatively structured activities were more effective than individually structured activities in promoting social interaction between mixed dyads of students
English, Goldstein, Shafer & Kaczmarek, 1997	multiple baseline	integrated preschool	8 children (5 typically developing)	50 days	Sensitivity training; peer strategy use training	Direct observation	◆ Significant increase in interactions between children after training
Evans, Salisbury, Palombaro & Berryman, 1992	descriptive study	inclusive elementary school	8 swsd and peers	1 school year	Examine social acceptance of students w/sd in inclusive classrooms	Assessment of Social Competence; sociometric analysis; classroom observation	◆ Students w/sd received more social approaches than they made ◆ Number of interaction declined over the year, but the patterns and types became more typical ◆ Acceptance was unrelated to social competence ◆ Social acceptance is not uniquely associated with disability status
Faught, Balleweg, Crow & van den Pol, 1983	descriptive study	integrated preschool program	12 students with and w/out disabilities	NS	Identify level and patterns of interaction among children	Direct observation	◆ Interaction between students with and without disabilities occurred about half of the time ◆ Typical children spent the largest proportion of their time with other typical children

Study	Design	Setting	Sample[1]	Duration[2]	Intervention/ Analysis	Data Sources	Findings
Fryxell & Kennedy, 1995	post-test only control group design	classes in inclusive schools; self-contained classes	18 swsd	4 months	Examine social relationships based on type of school placement	Direct observation; Social Network Form	◆ Students in gen ed placements had higher levels of social contact with peers ◆ Students in gen ed placements gave and received higher levels of social support ◆ Students in gen ed placements had larger friendships networks
Guralnick & Groom, 1988	treatment comparison	mainstreamed and specialized classroom setting	11 children with mild disabilities; 24 same age peers	2 years	Comparison of child behavior in two settings	Direct observation	◆ Higher levels of interaction and play associated with mainstreamed settings ◆ Proportion of typical children and availability of chronological age-peers important programmatic factors
Hamre-Nietupski, Hendrick-son, Nietupski & Shokoohi-Hekta, 1994	survey research	elementary, middle, and high schools in IA, NE, FL	312 gen ed teachers	1 round	Teacher responses to questions about friendship facilitation	Survey developed by authors	◆ Teachers felt friendships between diverse students possible ◆ Friendships should be facilitated by adults ◆ Friendships mutually beneficial to students ◆ Expressed high degree of willingness to use strategies to promote friendships between students

Study	Design	Setting	Sample[1]	Duration[2]	Intervention/ Analysis	Data Sources	Findings
Hanline, 1993	descriptive research	inclusive preschool	3 dyads of students with and without disabilities	4 weeks	Analysis of frequency and type of interactions occurring between children	Direct observation	◆ Children with disabilities had many opportunities to interact with peers ◆ Children with disabilities engaged in interactions comparable in length to those of their typical peers ◆ Typical children would benefit from help in understanding and responding to idiosyncratic behaviors of peers with disabilities
Hasazi, Gordon & Roe, 1985	descriptive research	9 Vermont school districts	462 students with disabilities	NS	Identify factors associated with employment status of students	Student records; interviews	◆ Over 50% of the sample was employed ◆ Most students found jobs in the self-family-friend network ◆ Paid employment in high school was a predictor of employment/ wages ◆ Students in resource room programs had higher employment rates than those placed in a special class
Hunt, Alwell, Farron-Davis & Goetz, 1996	multiple baseline design	1st and 4th grade classes	3 swsd and peers	1 school year	Multi-component package to facilitate social inclusion	Direct observation: Interactive Partnerships Scale; student interviews	◆ Increases were seen in reciprocal interactions and those initiated by the students w/sd ◆ Decreases in assisted interactions with paraprofessionals

Study	Design	Setting	Sample[1]	Duration[2]	Intervention/ Analysis	Data Sources	Findings
Hunt & Farron-Davis, 1992	Pre-test/posttest comparison design	Programs from seven states	11 teachers of swsd	1+ school year	Examined IEPs developed before and after placement in general ed classes	IEP Evaluation Instrument	◆ No differences found in curricular content before and after general class involvement ◆ Community-based opportunities did not decrease ◆ Quality of IEPs higher when students were members of general education class
Hunt, Farron-Davis, Beckstead, Curtis & Goetz, 1994	two-way small group design	8 inclusive programs; 8 self-contained programs	32 swd	NS	Comparison of student performance across settings	Direct observation; IEP analysis	◆ Important differences in the quality of written program plans for students with disabilities favoring those in inclusive settings ◆ Students in inclusive settings had higher levels of engagement in school activities, engaging in different types of activities than peers in self-contained classes ◆ Students with disabilities had higher levels of social interaction in inclusive programs
Hunt, Goetz & Anderson, 1986	Comparison study	4 Separate programs; 5 integrated programs	36 swsd	NS	Compare IEPs for students in segregated vs integrated programs	IEP Evaluation Instrument	◆ Quality of IEPs better for students placed in integrated school settings ◆ More opportunities for students in integrated programs

Study	Design	Setting	Sample[1]	Duration[2]	Intervention/ Analysis	Data Sources	Findings
Hunt, Staub, Alwell & Goetz, 1994	ABAB design	3 inclusive 2nd grade classrooms in San Francisco	students in these classes, including 3 swsd	10 weeks	Typical students were assisted to provide cues to students with disabilities to evoke target responses during a cooperative learning task	Direct observation of target motor, communication and academic skills	◆ 3 students with disabilities learned and generalized targeted skills ◆ Typical students in heterogeneous cooperative groups performed as well as students in groups without students with disabilities
Janney & Snell, 1996	ethnographic research	5 inclusive elementary schools	6 swsd and their peers	3 days/class	Identify strategies used by teachers to facilitate inclusion	Direct observation	◆ Teachers used typical peers in various ways to assist and promote interaction ◆ Classroom rules about helping changed ◆ The message "just another student" conferred membership status to student with disability ◆ Teachers encouraged age-appropriate interactions ◆ Teachers "backed off" when necessary to allow children to interact naturally

Study	Design	Setting	Sample[1]	Duration[2]	Intervention/ Analysis	Data Sources	Findings
Jenkins, Odom & Speltz, 1989	factorial design	integrated and non-integrated preschool classes	56 children with mild/ moderate disabilities	NS	Evaluate effects of both physical & social integration	Direct observation; standardized developmental measures	◆ Higher levels of interactive play and language development in social integration conditions ◆ Children in integrated settings received higher social competence ratings
Johnson & Johnson, 1981a	Group comparison	inner city elementary school	51 4th grade students with and w/out disabilities	16 days	Comparison of cooperative learning and individualistic learning on interpersonal attraction	Direct observation; nomination helping measure; participation measures	◆ Cooperative learning experiences promoted more interaction with students with disabilities during both instructional and free time situations ◆ Cooperative learning was associated with greater interpersonal attraction between students with and without disabilities
Johnson & Johnson, 1981b	Group comparison	suburban school district	40 3rd grade student with and w/out disabilities	16 days	Comparison of cooperative and individualistic learning conditions on friendships development	Direct observation; sociometric measure; attitude scales	◆ Cooperative learning experiences promote more friendships and interaction between students with and w/out disabilities within and outside of instructional situations

Study	Design	Setting	Sample[1]	Duration[2]	Intervention/ Analysis	Data Sources	Findings
Johnson, Johnson & Anderson, 1983	Survey research	districts in 3 different states	859 students, grades 4-9	single contact	Analysis of relationships between attitude measure and relationships with peers & teachers	Classroom Life Instrument (climate measure)	◆ Frequent participation in cooperative learning situations was positively related to perceptions of support, help, and friendship from teachers and peers
Johnson, Johnson, Tiffany & Zaidman, 1983	group comparison	inner city elementary school	48 ethnically diverse students in 4th grade	15 days of instruction	Comparison of cooperative and individualistic learning experiences with diverse students	Direct observation; measure of achievement; measure of perceived integration, interpersonal attraction; attitude scales	◆ Cooperative learning experiences promoted higher achievement for minority students, more cross-ethnic interaction, and greater cross-ethnic interpersonal attraction
Jolly, Test & Spooner, 1993	multiple baseline design	elementary school	2 swsd, 3 peers	5 months	Badges designating activity choices introduced to play sessions	Direct observation	◆ Use of badges resulted in greater frequency of positive play initiation and response behaviors

Study	Design	Setting	Sample[1]	Duration[2]	Intervention/ Analysis	Data Sources	Findings
Kennedy, Shukla & Fryxell, 1997	posttest-only control group design	self-contained and inclusive middle school class	16 swsd	1 school year	Comparison of social relationships based on educational placement	Direct observation; Social Contact Assessment Form; School-Based Social Network Form	◆ Substantial social benefits found for students in inclusive programs ◆ Students in gen ed settings interacted more frequently with peers ◆ Students in gen ed settings had larger and more durable peer networks
Kozleski & Jackson, 1993	longitudinal case study	elementary school	1 swsd, typical peers, teachers, parents	3 years	Examined experiences of educators and children as they participation in the full inclusion of a student w/sd	Interviews, sociometric measures, videotapes, direct observations	◆ Classroom teacher played a critical role in orchestrating the level of inclusion during a given year ◆ Over time, classmates initiated interaction outside of school ◆ Specific processes to support social relationships (e.g., Circle of Friends) were valuable ◆ Student experienced positive social relationships with her peers ◆ Improvement in communication skills and in other skills areas

Study	Design	Setting	Sample[1]	Duration[2]	Intervention/ Analysis	Data Sources	Findings
Lew, Mesch, Johnson & Johnson, 1986	Group comparison design	suburban school district	83 8th grade students; 4 students who were low achieving & socially isolated	21 weeks	Comparison of four conditions within cooperative learning groups	Measure of achievement, social interaction, and interpersonal attraction	◆ Positive goal interdependence with both collaborative skills & academic group contingencies promoted the most positive relationships with typical peer, most frequent engagement in cooperative skills, and the highest achievement
Logan, Bakeman & Keefe, 1997	descriptive study	29 classes in 4 elementary schools	29 swsd	3 months	Examine variables associated with the engaged behavior of swsd in general ed classes	Direct observation	◆ One-to-one, small group, and independent work arrangements were associated with higher engaged behavior than whole group instruction ◆ Swsd were almost twice as engaged in these settings
Maheady, Sacca & Harper, 1987	multiple baseline	9th & 10th grade math classes	29 students with mild disability; 63 typical peers	12 weeks	Use of classwide peer tutoring teams	Weekly math practice sheets and quizzes	◆ Average scores on weekly tests increase by 20 ◆ # of students earning A rose by 40% ◆ No students with disabilities failed

Study	Design	Setting	Sample[1]	Duration[2]	Intervention/ Analysis	Data Sources	Findings
McDonnell, Hardman, Hightower & Kiefer-O'Donnell, 1991	descriptive study	5 secondary programs	39 swsd	1 school year	Examined association between level of student integration and classroom & student characteristics	Student schedules; activity report logs; school demographic information; Scales of Independent Behavior	◆ Proximity of the student's placement to their home was positively associated with in-school and after school integration ◆ The number of students with severe disabilities at a school was negatively associated with in and after school integration ◆ Presence of intense behavior problems was negatively associated with after school integration ◆ Students placed in home school programs had significantly higher levels of integration than students enrolled in cluster programs

Study	Design	Setting	Sample[1]	Duration[2]	Intervention/Analysis	Data Sources	Findings
McDonnell, Thorson, McQuivey & Kiefer-O'Donnell, 1997	quasi-experimental between groups design	general education classroom	6 swsd; 12 typical peers	5 months	Compare levels of academic engagement of swsd and typical peers	Direct observation	(See Table B-2) ◆ Academic engagement rates of swsd were comparable to their typical peers in inclusive classrooms ◆ SWSD exhibited more competing behavior than their typical peers, but behaviors were not unlike those of their typical peers ◆ No significant differences in engagement rates were evident among swsd that were supported by paraprofessionals, and those who received support from peers
McDougall & Brady, 1998	multiple baseline	4th grade class	5 4th grade students - 2 with mild disabilities	44 sessions	Multi-component self-management intervention	Direct observation; performance in math sessions	◆ Students increased math fluency & engaged time after intervention faded ◆ 4/5 students matched or exceeded typical level of math fluency ◆ Students generalized improvements in math fluence ◆ Self-monitored accurately and punctually

Study	Design	Setting	Sample[1]	Duration[2]	Intervention/ Analysis	Data Sources	Findings
Meyer, Minondo, Fisher, Larson, Dunmore, Black & D'Aquanni, 1998	qualitative & quantitative methodologies for descriptive research	5 schools, ethnically & socially diverse	1-6 target swsd in each school; typical peers	1-3 school years	Construct social frames of interpersonal relationships	Student observation; family interviews; friendship survey; focus group interviews	◆ Six distinct frames were identified that characterize the social relationships of students with and without severe disabilities ◆ Frames are: ghosts and guests, the inclusion kid, I'll help, just another kid, regular friends, and best friends
Newton & Horner, 1993	multiple baseline design	apartment based residential program	staff and 3 people who lived in apt	25 weeks	Use of staff member as social guide to increase interaction	Valued Outcome Information System	◆ Increase in size of social networks ◆ Increase in frequency of social interaction ◆ Gains were generally maintained during a follow-up period
O'Connor & Jenkins, 1986	descriptive research	3 elementary schools	22 students with LD & matched typical peers	2 years	Describe experience of students with LD in cooperative learning groups	Direct observation;	◆ 40% of swd classified as successfully participating in cooperative groups ◆ Differences among classroom practices were related to successful cooperative learning experiences for swd
Odom & Strain, 1986	alternating treatment design	classroom in preschool	3 preschool children with autism	40 sessions	Comparison of two procedures for improving social interaction	Direct observation; peer questionnaire	◆ Both teacher and peer interventions were successful in increasing social responses of students w/sd ◆ Teacher condition also produced increased level of responding among children

Study	Design	Setting	Sample[1]	Duration[2]	Intervention/ Analysis	Data Sources	Findings
Putnam, Rynders, Johnson & Johnson, 1989	group comparison design	elementary school	16 swsd and 32 typical peers	NS	Explicit instruction on collaborative skills as part of cooperatively structured activities	Direct observation	◆ Students who received collaborative skill instruction interacted more positively than those who didn't ◆ Instruction had greatest impact upon behaviors directed toward students with disabilities
Sale & Carey, 1995	sociometric descriptive study	inclusive elementary school	all students in school	NS	Examine socio-metric status of students w/d in inclusive school	Peer nomination data	◆ Students with disabilities had lower peer preference scores than their general education peers
Salisbury, Evans & Palombaro, 1997	qualitative study	inclusive elementary school	Students in grades K-4	2 years	Impact of collaborative problem solving	Videotape, audiotape, written records, direct observations, teacher interviews	◆ Process was successfully implemented as designed in 12 classrooms ◆ Teachers judged CPS to be easily incorporated into existing practices ◆ CPS promoted outcomes valued by administrators, teachers, & parents

Study	Design	Setting	Sample[1]	Duration[2]	Intervention/ Analysis	Data Sources	Findings
Salisbury, Gallucci, Palombaro & Peck, 1995	qualitative study	two inclusive elementary schools	10 general ed teachers	at least 6 months	Studied strategies used by general ed teachers to promote positive relationships between students	Direct observation; interviews with general ed teachers	◆ Five strategies used by classroom teachers were identified ◆ Strategies were: active facilitation of interactions, empowering children, building sense of community, modeling acceptance, and developing school organizational supports
Salisbury & Palombaro, 1998	ethnographic approach	elementary school	3 swsd in inclusive elementary school	2 yrs	Analysis of friendship patterns	Field notes; social standing assessment; teacher interviews	◆ Friendships patterns differed across three students studied, although all experienced physical, social & instructional inclusion ◆ Severity of disability did not preclude the formation of social relations and interactions with peers ◆ Teachers employed proactive strategies to support interaction, but did not force friendships

Study	Design	Setting	Sample[1]	Duration[2]	Intervention/ Analysis	Data Sources	Findings
Sapon-Shevin, Dobbelaere, Corrigan, Goodman & Mastin, 1998	qualitative	elementary school	students in grades K-4	3+ school years	Implemented rule "You can't say you can't play" in four classrooms	Transcripts of teachers' meeting; teacher interviews; observer field notes; student interviews; teacher manuscripts	◆ Rule was positive organizing principle for classrooms ◆ Rule was powerful in changing behavior in context in which teachers already took seriously their roles in structuring social interactions between students ◆ Rule was not a cure-all ◆ Rule provided basis for discussion and analysis of situations arising in the school & classroom
Sasso & Rude, 1987	counter-balanced withdrawal design	elementary school play-ground	8 pairs of student w/wout disabilities	7 weeks	Use of high & low status peers to encourage others to interact with students w/d	Direct observation	◆ Interaction of high-status peer resulted in higher levels of initiations by untrained peers ◆ Social response levels differentially affected by status of the peer initiator
Schnorr, 1997	ethnographic research	urban school district	middle & high school students in 4 general ed classes	1 semester	Examined meaning of "belonging" in four general ed classes	Participation observations; semi-structured interviews	◆ Student membership depends upon on affiliation with a subgroup of peers within the class ◆ Only some of the students with disabilities connected with subgroups and were considered class members

Study	Design	Setting	Sample[1]	Duration[2]	Intervention/ Analysis	Data Sources	Findings
Schnorr, 1990	qualitative study	first grade classroom	23 first graders; 1 student who was main-streamed	1 school year	Examine what typical students think about their school experience & mainstreamed student	Direct observation; student interviews	◆ First graders have common framework for defining their school experience ◆ Significant discrepancies between the students' definitions of what it means to be part of first grade and Peter's involvement in the class
Staub, Schwartz, Gallucci & Peck, 1994	case study	inclusive elementary school	4 hetero-geneous pairs of students	1 school year	Construct "portraits" of the friendships between students	Observation, videotapes, interviews	(see Table B-2,B-3) ◆ All four students had rich and varied relationships ◆ All four friendships had roots in nontutorial contexts and activities ◆ Classrooms teachers used strategies to actively promote interaction
Strain & Odom, 1986	alternating treatment design	integrated preschool	3 swsd; 4 typical peers	40 sessions	Comparison of peer-initiation and teacher-antecedent interventions for promoting interaction	Direct observation	◆ Both approaches increased initiation of social responses ◆ Teacher-antecedent approach also produced increases in responses to social initiations

Study	Design	Setting	Sample[1]	Duration[2]	Intervention/ Analysis	Data Sources	Findings
Tralli, Colombo, Deshler & Schumaker, 1996	case study descriptions	secondary schools in CT and MO	2 high schools	7 years; 2 years	Implementation of Strategies Intervention Model	Key staff in buildings	◆ Process of building support takes time and a broad base of support ◆ Each example indicates need for "supported inclusion", not simply placement, to achieve meaningful student outcomes
Wang & Birch, 1984	pre-test/ post-test group comparison	elementary school	179 students	1 school year	Comparison of student progress across settings	Student achievement measures; Perceived Competence Scale ; program cost records	◆ ALEM program model resulted in greater performance, attitudes, and participation of swd ◆ Costs projections suggest program is less expensive than traditional special education model across time
Wehman, Kregel & Seyfarth, 1985	survey research	Virginia	117 transition aged swsd	single contact	Assess employment status of swsd after leaving school	Responses to survey questions	◆ There was an 88% unemployment rate for this sample of former students ◆ A number of respondents did not have many years of special education services ◆ Poor employment and wage outcomes seen as outcomes of school programs that incorporated little functional community-based training

Study	Design	Setting	Sample[1]	Duration[2]	Intervention/ Analysis	Data Sources	Findings
Zigmond & Baker, 1990	pre-test/ post-test design	urban elementary school	13 students with LD	2 years	MELD model	Classroom Behavior measure; school adjustment measures; standardized achievement; curriculum-based measure	◆ MELD model was not fully incorporated into mainstreamed classes ◆ Students with disabilities adjusted well to general ed classrooms ◆ Students made no significant progress in reading or math, and earned lower grades in implementation year

[1]Abbreviations: swsd = student(s) with severe disabilities; swd - student with a disability; w/wout - with and without NS = not specified.

Table B-2
Documented Outcomes for Students without Disabilities in Inclusive Settings

Study	Design	Setting	Sample[1]	Duration[2]	Intervention/ Analysis	Data Sources	Findings
Bricker, Bruder & Bailey, 1982	pre-test/ post-test comparison	3 develop-mentally integrated classes	16 children w/wout disabilities	1 school year	Effects of integration on children w/wout disabilities	Norm & criterion-referenced developmental measures; index of educational significance	◆ Students w/out disabilities made significant progress on all measures but one, not expected to change if child is within normal range ◆ Students with disabilities made significant progress on all measures as above ◆ Integration beneficial for both groups of students
Dugan, Kamps, Leonard, Watkins, Rheinberger & Stackhaus, 1995	ABAB design	4th grade social studies class	2 students with autism; 16 4th grade peers	13 weeks	Use of cooperative learning groups	Weekly social studies pre and post tests; direct observation	◆ Academic gains for both target student and peers ◆ Intervention associated with increased academic engagement and duration of student interaction
Evans, Salisbury, Palombaro & Goldberg, 1994	post-test only design	inclusive elementary school	50 children, K-2	single session	Students were read simple stores about common incidents that might occur	Student responses to structured interview questions	◆ Students demonstrated sophisticated understanding of concepts of fairness and equity

Study	Design	Setting	Sample[1]	Duration[2]	Intervention/ Analysis	Data Sources	Findings
Giangreco, Edelman, Cloninger, & Dennis, 1993c	survey research	inclusive public schools	81 parents with non-disabled children, K-3	single contact	Parent perceptions about impact of inclusive approaches on typical children	Parents of students without disabilities	◆ Parents report direct positive influence on child's development as a result of inclusive educational experiences ◆ Children feel comfortable interacting with child with severe disabilities ◆ Parents reported children experience social emotional growth ◆ Child feels positively about having classmate wsd
Helmstetter, Peck & Giangreco, 1994	survey research	45 high schools in WA state	166 high school students	single contact	Survey that examines benefits and difficulties of relationships with students with severe disabilities	Student response to survey items	◆ Seven different types of positive outcomes associated with interaction with students with disabilities were reported by high school students ◆ Outcomes were not affected by gender, grade, setting, or amount of contact with peers with disabilities outside of school ◆ Amount of contact within the school setting was positively associated with outcomes ◆ Type of contact also associated with outcomes, i.e., the more direct the contact, the more positive the outcomes reported

Study	Design	Setting	Sample[1]	Duration[2]	Intervention/ Analysis	Data Sources	Findings
Hollowood, Salisbury, Rainforth & Palombaro, 1994/1995	causal-comparative between groups design	8 classes in inclusive elementary school	6 swsd; 12 students w/out disabilities	5 months	Comparison of engaged time in classes with and w/out swsd	Direct observation; teacher lesson plans; schedules	◆ Settings differences were not found for engaged time measures ◆ Students with severe disabilities had no effect on losses of instructional time
Hunt, Staub, Alwell & Goetz, 1994	ABAB design	3 inclusive 2nd grade classrooms in San Francisco	students in these classes, including 3 swsd	10 weeks	Typical students were assisted to provide cues to students with disabilities to evoke target responses during a cooperative learning task	Direct observation of target motor, communication and academic skills	◆ 3 students with disabilities learned and generalized targeted skills ◆ Typical students in heterogeneous cooperative groups performed as well as students in groups without students with disabilities
Kishi & Meyer, 1994	group comparison design	Hawaii public schools	183 students aged 15-19	6 year follow-up study	Comparison of response between contact (Special Friends), exposure and control group	Acceptance Scale; Self-Observation Scale; student interviews	◆ Students with more involvement as young children reported most contact with people with disabilities at this time ◆ Contact was associated with higher levels of self-acceptance, self-security, and self-assertion ◆ Early contact was associated with higher levels of support for community participation

Study	Design	Setting	Sample[1]	Duration[2]	Intervention/ Analysis	Data Sources	Findings
Lowenbraun Madge & Affleck, 1990	survey research	Issaquah School District (WA)	134 parents of students in integrated classes	single contact; report about 6 month period	Comparison of satisfaction ratings of parents of student w/wout disabilities	Questionnaire	◆ Majority of parents of typical students satisfied with placement and child progress, and would choose such a placement in the future ◆ Majority of parents of swd were satisfied with placement ◆ Among parents with prior resource room experience, comparably positive ratings were given to both placements ◆ Resource room rated lower relative to academic progress and self-esteem
McDonnell, Thorson, McQuivey & Kiefer-O'Donnell, 1997	quasi-experiential between groups design	general education classroom	6 students w/sd; 12 students w/out disabilities	5 months	Compare levels of academic engagement of swsd and typical peers	Direct observation	(See Table B-1) ◆ Typical students in inclusive classrooms had comparable engagement levels to peers in classes without swsd
McDougall & Bradey, 1998	multiple baseline	4th grade classroom	5 4th grade students - 2 with mild disabilities	44 sessions	Multi-component self-management intervention	Direct observation; performance in math sessions	◆ Students increased math fluency & engaged time after intervention faded ◆ 4/5 students matched or exceeded typical level of math fluency ◆ Students generalized improvements in math fluence ◆ Self-monitored accurately and punctually

Study	Design	Setting	Sample[1]	Duration[2]	Intervention/ Analysis	Data Sources	Findings
Odom, Deklyen & Jenkins, 1984	pre-test/post-test group comparison	preschool	32 children w/out disabilities	1 school year	Comparison of developmental gains across settings	Developmental assessments; teacher rating assessment	◆ No significant differences were found between groups of children ◆ Placement in settings in which a majority of students were typically developing poses no developmental risks
Peck, Carlson & Helmstetter, 1992	survey research	integrated preschool and kinder-garten classes	125 parents of typical children and 95 teachers	single contact	Describe perceptions of parents & gen ed teachers about inclusive programs	Responses to semi-structured interview	◆ Both parents and teachers reported benefits to typical children as a result of these programs ◆ Common concerns about integration not generally perceived as problems by respondents
Peck, Donaldson & Pezzoli, 1990	qualitative research	high school in ID and CA	21 typical high school students	single contact	Investigate benefits of involvement with swsd	Semi-structured interviews	◆ Student responses described six types of benefits from their relationships with swsd ◆ Benefits include: self-concept; social-cognitive growth; reduced fear of human differences; increased tolerance; principles of personal conduct; and relaxed & accepting friendships ◆ Areas of difficulty in these relationships typically involved responses to inappropriate behavior

Study	Design	Setting	Sample[1]	Duration[2]	Intervention/ Analysis	Data Sources	Findings
Sharpe, York & Knight, 1994	pre-test/ post-test post hoc study	elementary school	143 typical students	3 school years	Comparison of performance of student in inclusive and non-inclusive classrooms	SRA Assessment Survey; Houghton Mifflin Book Placement; report cards	◆ No significant differences between groups on any measure
Staub & Hunt, 1993	multiple baseline design	special education classroom	4 swsd; 8 typical peer tutors	30 days	Social interaction training provided to 4 of 8 peer tutors	Direct observation	◆ Training increased the frequency of interactions directed from peer tutors towards swsd ◆ Increase in social interactions ◆ Increase in targeted social behaviors of swsd
Staub, Schwartz, Gallucci & Peck, 1994	case study	inclusive elementary school	4 hetero-geneous pairs of students	1 school year	Construct "portraits" of the friendships between students	Observation; videotapes; interviews	(see Tables B-1,B-3) ◆ Typical students received support and recognition for their friendships from school personnel

Study	Design	Setting	Sample[1]	Duration[2]	Intervention/ Analysis	Data Sources	Findings
Staub, Spaulding, Peck, Gallucci & Schwartz, 1996	qualitative study	inclusive junior high school	4 swsd; 31 typical students	2 school years	Describe how one school includes students; outcomes of student aide program	Direct observation; semi-structured interviews	◆ Building a philosophy & leadership were critical to success of inclusion ◆ Use of typical students to support swsd resulted in greater independence, social & behavioral growth ◆ Benefits for typical students included increased social networks, improved self-esteem, and greater awareness and appreciation of people with disabilities
York & Tundidor, 1995	focus group and qualitative methodology	urban school district	335 general & special educators, administrators, support staff, parents & students	2 years	Develop district profile of the issues raised when moving toward more inclusive service model	45 focus group discussions	(See Table B-3, B-4) ◆ Student reportedly received little information about disabilities and how to interact with swd ◆ Students engaged in discussions about how they could facilitate greater inclusion of their peers with disabilities ◆ Students were more open to greater degrees of inclusion than the adults

[1]Abbreviations: swsd = student(s) with severe disabilities; swd - student with a disability; w/wout - with and without NS = not specified.

Table B-3
Documented Outcomes for Parents Associated with Inclusive Settings

Study	Design	Setting	Sample[1]	Duration[2]	Intervention/ Analysis	Data Sources	Findings
Bailey & Winton, 1989	Descriptive study	university day care center	47 parents of young children	1 school year	Describe changes in friendship and acquaintance patterns over time	Sociometric rating instrument; two other rating scales	◆ Families of children with disabilities attending mainstreamed day care center more likely to meet and become friends with other families of children with disabilities ◆ All parents got to know more parents of typically developing children over time, but parents of children with disabilities were less likely to know others outside their group ◆ Parents of children with disabilities less satisfied with their acquaintance with other families
Bailey & Winton, 1987	survey research	preschool	parents of all children at Frank Porter Graham Child Development Ctr	9 months	Describe parents expectations about inclusive programs across time	Parent interviews	◆ Response patterns among parents of students with and without disabilities were similar ◆ Parent expectations about programmatic benefits did not change across time ◆ For parents of typical children, some prior concerns were not realized

Study	Design	Setting	Sample[1]	Duration[2]	Intervention/ Analysis	Data Sources	Findings
Bennett, DeLuca & Bruns, 1997	descriptive research	preschool & elementary schools	84 teachers; 48 parents	single contact	Examine perspectives of teachers & parents	Survey responses; interviews with sub-sample of participants	◆ Parents reported strong feelings about the benefits of inclusion for their child ◆ Parents reported generally positive experiences with inclusion ◆ Inclusion facilitated the development of friendships outside of school
Diamond & LeFurgy, 1994	survey research	Integrated and self-contained preschool classes	141 parents of young children	2 school years	Compare responses of parents based on child's placement	Parent Perspectives on Integration Questionnaire	◆ All parents held generally positive views about integration ◆ Parents who had participated in integrated classes held more positive attitudes than those who didn't
Giangreco, Cloninger, Mueller, Yuan & Ashworth, 1991	qualitative research	public schools in VT	28 families of students with dual sensory impairments	single contact	Investigate parent perceptions of educational & related services	Parent interviews	◆ Four areas dominated parent thinking: a "good life" for their child; experiences with fear, frustration; and change ◆ Parents want professionals to listen to them and trust them ◆ Parents want a stable educational program (not moved from year to year) ◆ Parents want professional to be honest with them

Study	Design	Setting	Sample[1]	Duration[2]	Intervention/Analysis	Data Sources	Findings
Green & Shinn, 1994	survey research	6 urban elementary schools in the Pacific Northwest	parents of 21 students receiving resource services	single contact	Examine what and how parents think about special ed services and reintegration	Parent interviews	◆ Most parents had strong positive feelings about resource room services ◆ Parental satisfaction based on subjective feels about program rather than academic performance data ◆ Most parents reluctant to have child placed in general education classrooms
Green & Stoneman, 1989	survey research	day care and preschool settings	204 parents of typical young children with disabilities	single contact	Examine perspective of parents of typical children toward mainstreaming	Parent Attitudes Toward Mainstreaming Scale	◆ Parents who had previous experiences with integrated programs had more positive attitudes than parents who didn't ◆ Parents of young preschool children held more positive attitudes toward integration than parents of older children ◆ Parents expressed greatest concern about integrating children with severe mental retardation, emotional disturbance, or behavior problems

Study	Design	Setting	Sample[1]	Duration[2]	Intervention/ Analysis	Data Sources	Findings
Guralnick, Connor & Hammond, 1995	survey research	integrated & specialized preschool programs in large metropoli-tan community	262 mothers of at-risk and preschool children with disabilities	single contact	Investigate parent perspectives of peer relationships and friendships in integrated & specialized programs	Child Behavior Checklist; parent interviews	◆ Mothers of children in both types of settings perceive programs as valuable ◆ Mothers of children in integrated settings report gains in play and social skills due to presence of typical children ◆ Both groups of mothers were concerned about peer rejection, and noted the importance of other children with special needs
Hamre-Nietupski, 1993	survey research	one Area Education Agency in IA	53 parents of swsd	single contact	Examine differences among parents based on level of disability of child; how should instructional time be used	Survey responses	◆ All parents reported preference for largest % of school day to be spent on functional skill instruction ◆ Second highest preference of parents of swsd was social relationship development ◆ Trend toward increase in support for functional life skills as age of student increases

Study	Design	Setting	Sample[1]	Duration[2]	Intervention/ Analysis	Data Sources	Findings
Hamre-Nietupski, Nietupski & Strathe, 1992	survey research	regional education district in IA	68 parents of swsd	single contact	Identify educational activity preferences of parents	Survey responses	◆ Parents of students with moderate disabilities placed greater emphasis on functional life skills over social relationships ◆ Parents of students with severe/profound disabilities rated social relationships most highly
McDonnell, 1987	survey, research	schools with both integrated and separate programs	400 parents of swsd	single contact	Comparison of responses of parents based on placement of their child	Survey responses	◆ Significant differences in perceptions of two parent groups on all variables ◆ Parents of children in integrated settings overwhelmingly positive ◆ Parents of children in segregated settings predicted integrated placement would be negative
Miller, Strain, Boyd, Hunsicker, McKinley & Wu, 1992	survey research	mainstreamed & segregated preschool programs	230 parents	1st year results of 5 year study	Extend findings of studies comparing parent perceptions about integrated preschool programs	Parent Opinion Surveys 1 & 2	◆ Parents of both groups held high opinions of mainstreaming ◆ Parents of typical children & children with disabilities in mainstreamed settings felt more strongly about the positive impact of this experience on their children

Study	Design	Setting	Sample[1]	Duration[2]	Intervention/ Analysis	Data Sources	Findings
Palmer, Borthwick-Duffy & Widaman, 1998	survey research	special day classes in Los Angeles	460 parents	single contact	Examine parent perspectives about inclusion	Parent response to surveys	◆ Parents of students served in self-contained settings positive about potential social benefits, acceptance, and treatment of their child in inclusive settings ◆ Parents were more apprehensive about program quality in inclusive settings
Reichart, Lynch, Anderson, Svobodny, DiCola & Mercury, 1989	survey research	early childhood special ed program; traditional early childhood program	51 parents of young children	single contact	Compare perspectives of parents based on child's placement	Parent Perspective on Integration	◆ Both groups of parents held positive perspectives about integration ◆ Few concerns were reported about the effects of integration of their child or the program structure ◆ All parents identified teacher training in early childhood and special education as important to integrated program
Staub, Schwartz, Gallucci & Peck, 1994 (see Table B-1)	case study	inclusive elementary school	4 hetero-geneous pairs of students	1 school year	Construct "portraits" of the friendships between students	Observation, videotapes, interviews	(see Table B-1,B-2) ◆ Parents of the students without disabilities were highly supportive of inclusion

Study	Design	Setting	Sample[1]	Duration[2]	Intervention/ Analysis	Data Sources	Findings
Turnbull & Winton, 1983	survey research	specialized preschool; main-streamed preschool	mothers of 31 children with disabilities	NS	Compare perspectives of mothers based on child's placement	Face to face interview; telephone questionnaire	◆ Mother's perception of child's needs and their own needs influenced their choice of preschools ◆ All parents looking for placement to enhance child's development ◆ Parents of children in mainstream setting placed greater importance on normal peer interaction ◆ Parents of children in specialized setting placed greater emphasis on professional involvement, providing parents with time for themselves
Turnbull, Winton, Blacher & Salkind, 1982	survey research	main-streamed kindergart-en	101 parents of children with and w/out disabilities	single contact	Comparison of perspectives of parents of children with and w/out disabilities	Response during telephone interview	◆ High level of agreement across groups of parents ◆ Parents identified social outcomes as greatest benefit ◆ Greatest drawbacks identified related to instructional issues ◆ Parents needed more information about mainstreaming

Study	Design	Setting	Sample[1]	Duration[2]	Intervention/ Analysis	Data Sources	Findings
York & Tundidor, 1995	focus group and qualitative methodology	urban school district	335 general & special educators, adminis-trators, support staff, parents & students	2 years	Develop district profile of the issues raised when moving toward more inclusive service model	45 focus group discussions	(see Table B-4, B-2) ◆ Parents in focus group identified negative attitudes of professional staff as a barrier to inclusion ◆ Parents concerned with protecting their children from intentional and unintentional psychological & physical harm

[1]Abbreviations: swsd = student(s) with severe disabilities; swd - student with a disability; w/wout - with and without NS = not specified.

Table B-4
Outcomes and Behaviors of Teachers in Inclusive Settings

Study	Design	Setting	Sample[1]	Duration[2]	Intervention/ Analysis	Data Sources	Findings
Bennett, DeLuca & Bruns, 1997	descriptive research	preschool & elementary schools	84 teachers; 48 parents	single contact	Examine perspectives of teachers & parents	Survey responses; interviews with sub-sample of participants	◆ Teachers reported moderate level of confidence in their ability to implement inclusive practices ◆ Experience in including students was positively related to confidence in skills to successfully do so ◆ The amount of training received by teachers is positively related to teacher confidence and attitudes about inclusion
Billingsley & Kelly, 1994	survey research	NS	53 profess-ionals & research personnel	single contact	Determine viability of instructional procedures in general ed settings	Survey responses	◆ Of 51 effective instructional practices, 12 were considered inappropriate in general ed settings by 20% of more respondents ◆ The most frequent reason for a practice to be judged in-appropriate was logistical

Study	Design	Setting	Sample[1]	Duration[2]	Intervention/ Analysis	Data Sources	Findings
Brady, Swank, Taylor & Freiberg, 1992	control group factorial design	3 districts in the Houston area	35 teachers, 6-8th grade social studies & science	1 semester	6 session inservice emphasizing teacher effectiveness variables	Direct observation	◆ Significant differences were seen between trained teachers and those in the control group ◆ Mainstreamed students received more guidance from teachers than other students ◆ Science teachers showed greater positive changes than social studies teachers
Ferguson, Meyer, Janchild, Juniper & Zingo, 1992	qualitative study	3 elementary 3 middle & 6 high schools	NS	2 years	Examine role of teacher in facilitating inclusion	Direct observation; interviews	◆ Inclusion facilitated by three types of supports: teaching, prosthetic & interpretive ◆ Inclusion facilitated by working flexibly between curricular infusion, learning inclusion, and social inclusion ◆ Collaborative and consultative teacher relationships important

Study	Design	Setting	Sample[1]	Duration[2]	Intervention/ Analysis	Data Sources	Findings
Gemmel-Crosby & Hanzlik, 1994	survey research	private preschools in mid-sized cities	79 preschool teachers	single contact	Examine perspectives about inclusion	Survey responses	◆ The more satisfied teachers were with the level of support and training received, the more positive their attitudes ◆ Teachers with greater confidence about teaching students with disabilities had more positive attitudes toward inclusion ◆ Feelings of competency were positively correlated with adequacy of support & training
Giangreco, Dennis, Cloninger, Edelman & Schattman, 1993b	qualitative study	Vermont public schools, K-9	19 general ed teachers	4 months	Describe the experiences of general ed teachers who are including a swsd	Semi-structured teacher interviews	◆ Despite initial negative reactions to placement of swsd, 17 teachers changed their opinions over time ◆ Teachers identified many benefits to students and themselves ◆ Teamwork was viewed as an important support ◆ Presence of many specialists reported to be unhelpful
Giangreco, Edelman, Luiselli & MacFarland, 1997	qualitative study	11 schools in CT, MA, UT, VT	16 classes	2 school years	Examine effects of teaching assistant on students supported in gen ed classes	Direct observation	◆ Potential negative effects of high levels of physical proximity of instructional assistant to student w/sd in gen ed classes are identified ◆ 8 potential areas of negative impact are identified

Study	Design	Setting	Sample[1]	Duration[2]	Intervention/ Analysis	Data Sources	Findings
Hamre-Nietupski, Hendrickson, Nietupski, Sasso, 1993	survey research	schools in IA, NE, and FL	158 special ed teachers	single contact	Explore perceptions of teachers regarding friendship facilitation	Survey responses	◆ Teachers believe friendships are possible and they should be facilitated ◆ Teachers believe involvement in general ed classrooms is critical ◆ Responsibility falls to teachers and parents to facilitate friendships ◆ Most effective strategies involve collaboration, presentation of information, cooperative learning, peer tutoring, and social skills training
Janney & Snell, 1996	ethnographic research	5 inclusive elementary schools	6 swsd and their peers	3 days/ class	Identify strategies used by teachers to facilitate inclusion	Direct observation	◆ Teachers used typical peers in various ways to assist and promote interaction ◆ Classroom rules about helping changed ◆ The message "just another student" conferred membership status to student with disability ◆ Teachers encouraged age-appropriate interactions ◆ Teachers "backed off" when necessary to allow children to interact naturally

Study	Design	Setting	Sample[1]	Duration[2]	Intervention/Analysis	Data Sources	Findings
Janney, Snell, Beers & Raynes, 1995	qualitative	5 Virginia school districts	53 teachers and administrators	30-90 minute inter-views	Gather advice from experienced practitioners	Semi-structured interviews	◆ Participants felts benefits outweigh "costs" of inclusive practices ◆ Advice provided for teachers and administrators regarding attitudes, strategies, and necessary supports
Logan, Bakerman & Keefe, 1997	descriptive study	29 classes in 4 elementary schools	29 swsd	3 months	Examine variables associated with the engaged behavior of swsd in general ed classes	Direct observation	◆ One-to-one, small group, and independent work arrangements were associated with higher engaged behavior than whole group instruction ◆ Students were almost twice as engaged in these settings
Olson, Chalmers & Hoover, 1997	survey research	Grand Forks metropolitan area	10 general educators, elem & secondary	single contact	Perceptions of effective inclusionists	Teacher interviews	◆ Teachers described themselves as tolerant, reflective and flexible, & willing to accept responsibility for all students ◆ Teachers had a positive relationship with the special educator ◆ Reported insufficient time for collaboration, and reservations about including all students

Study	Design	Setting	Sample[1]	Duration[2]	Intervention/ Analysis	Data Sources	Findings
Pugach & Johnson, 1995	group comparison study	schools in WI, IL, AL	191 teachers	1 school year	Use of structured dialogue strategies taught to teachers	# of referrals; demographic questionnaire; Teachable Pupil Survey; Teacher Efficacy Scale; Classroom Questionnaire; Classroom Problem Questionnaire	◆ Intervention group had reduced referral rates, increased confidence in handling classroom problems, increased positive teacher affect toward the classroom, and greater tolerance about cognitive deficits ◆ Teachers were able to solve 88% of the classroom problems encountered
Salend, Johansen, Mumper, Chase, Pike & Dorney, 1997	qualitative research	kinder-garten class in elementary school	2 coopera-ting teachers	1 school year	Examine perspectives and experiences of co-teachers	Teacher journals; teacher interviews	◆ After initial difficulties, teachers began to respect, recognize & utilize their mutual strengths ◆ Both teachers expressed great satisfaction at the end of the year ◆ Commitment to teaming was related to social & academic growth of the students
Werts, Wolery, Snyder, Caldwell & Salisbury, 1996	survey research	national sampling	1,491 general ed teachers, K-6	single contact	Identify perceptions and needs of general ed teachers	Survey responses	◆ Teachers with students included in their classroom reported needs that exceeded the available of supports ◆ Discrepancies between reported need and availability of support were greater for teachers with students who with more severe disabilities

Study	Design	Setting	Sample[1]	Duration[2]	Intervention/ Analysis	Data Sources	Findings
Wolery, Anthony, Snyder, Werts & Katzen-meyer, 1997	multiple probe design	3 suburban elementary schools	3 general ed teachers; swsd in each class	40 sessions	Evaluate effects of training package to teach teachers to use constant time delay strategy	Direct observation; teacher interviews	◆ Training resulted in correct & frequent use of constant time delay during general ed instruction ◆ Student performance increased in response to this instruction ◆ Two of the three teachers reported to like the strategy
Wolery, Werts, Caldwell, Snyder & Liskowski, 1995	survey research	elementary schools in PA	158 elementary teachers	single contact	Identify supports available to them for inclusion	Teacher survey responses	◆ Special & general educators reported similar levels of resource needs ◆ A high percentage of respondents reported unmet training needs ◆ Most teachers reported sufficient access to support personnel ◆ Teachers reporting success with inclusion had less unmet needs
Wood, 1998	qualitative research	inclusive elementary classes	3 teams, consisting of parent, child, general ed & special ed teacher	4 months	Investigate teachers' perceptions of their educational roles in an inclusive school	Teacher interviews	◆ During initial stages of inclusion, teachers maintained discrete role boundaries ◆ As school year progressed, role perceptions became less rigid and teaming more cooperative

Study	Design	Setting	Sample[1]	Duration[2]	Intervention/ Analysis	Data Sources	Findings
York & Tundidor, 1995	focus group & qualitative methodology	urban school district	335 general & special ed teachers, administrators, support staff, parents & students	2 years	Develop district profile of the issues raised when moving toward more inclusive mode	45 focus group discussions	◆ Positive attitudes & cooperation among staff facilitate inclusion ◆ Priorities include inservice training, time for collaboration & increased parent involvement ◆ Clear definition of inclusion needed ◆ Rigid general ed curricular options represent barrier to inclusion
York, Vandercook, MacDonald, Heise-Neff & Caughey, 1992	survey research	2 middle schools; Twin Cities, MN	11 general ed teachers; 7 special ed teachers; 181 middle school students	single contact, end of school year	Feedback after initial year of integrating swsd in general ed classes	Survey responses	◆ Teachers and students reported increases in social competence of swsd ◆ Student acceptance of classmates increased over the year ◆ Teachers generally felt positive about the experience ◆ Area of greatest difficulty was deciding how to involve the students

[1]Abbreviations: swsd = student(s) with severe disabilities; swd - student with a disability; w/wout - with and without NS = not specified.

Table B-5
Programmatic and Administrative Outcomes of Inclusive Schooling

Study	Design	Setting	Sample[1]	Duration[2]	Intervention/ Analysis	Data Sources	Findings
McLaughlin & Warren, 1994	descriptive study with cross-site analysis	IL, NY, WA, VA, NM, VT, CO, MD	14 school districts	NS	Obtain information about costs of inclusion	Interviews with special ed directors, principals, and other administrators	◆ Relatively little change in the # of professional special educators employed was noted across 14 sites ◆ Special education personnel were used differently ◆ Instructional assistants have more direct student responsibilities ◆ Some suburban & urban districts reported savings in transportation costs ◆ Most frequent renovations reported involved restrooms, ramps, and curb cuts ◆ Need for more group space for teachers ◆ All districts invested heavily in staff development ◆ Inclusion did cost more initially in this sample of districts, but is not likely to be more expensive to maintain

Study	Design	Setting	Sample[1]	Duration[2]	Intervention/ Analysis	Data Sources	Findings
Pugach & Johnson, 1995	group comparison study	schools in WI, IL, AL	191 teachers	1 school years	Use of structured dialogue strategies taught to teachers	# of referrals; demographic questionnaire; Teachable Pupil Survey; Teacher Efficacy Scale; Classroom Questionnaire; Classroom Problem Questionnaire	(See Table B-4) ◆ Peer collaboration model resulted in lower special education referral rates
Salisbury, Wilson, Swartz, Palombaro & Wassel, 1997	action research	Fox Chapel, PA; Johnson City, NY	31 swsd across two years; 52 staff members across 2 yrs	2 years	Examine use of action research as a strategy to solve instructional problems in inclusive settings	Direct observation; child performance measures; Classroom Environment Scale	◆ Teachers report positive outcomes for themselves and students as a result of action research projects ◆ Action research is effective in improving the quality of professional practice and in helping teachers to become more reflective